THE MAKING OF MODERN
ENGLISH RELIGION

THE
MAKING OF MODERN
ENGLISH RELIGION

*An historical impression of certain
religious forces in modern English history*

BY

BERNARD LORD MANNING
Fellow of Jesus College, Cambridge

LONDON
INDEPENDENT PRESS
LIVINGSTONE HOUSE, SW1

Made and Printed in England by
Clare, Son & Co Ltd, (British Printing Corporation) Wells, Somerset

TO

MY FATHER AND MY MOTHER

Jerusalem pacifera,
Haec tibi sunt fundamenta.
Felix et Deo proxima
Quae te meretur anima;
Custos tuarum turrium
Non dormit in perpetuum.

CONTENTS

FOREWORD

BERNARD MANNING was one of the greatest defenders of the Faith both by his life and his teaching. What C. S. Lewis, Dorothy Sayers and T. S. Eliot were to the Christian Faith and the Church of England, what G. K. Chesterton and Hilaire Belloc were to the Christian Faith and the Church of Rome, Bernard Manning was to the Christian Faith and Orthodox Dissent,[1] and many who knew him and still cherish his writings would say, without fear of exaggeration, that even in that distinguished company he was the most Christian, the wittiest, and the most discerning and persuasive of them all.

The reader must try Manning for himself. He will be delighted by his wit and felicity of illustration, instructed in the central truths of the Faith and made wise in churchmanship by his piety and acute common sense, and be grateful for a writer who had so much to say to his own and to this generation.

But if his writings are so good, why should he be unknown today? Some explanations may be given. First, he was an invalid with tuberculosis, living on one lung from childhood. He had little energy to spare for writing so his output was not large, and after his regular work was done, he had no energy left to make himself a national figure. Secondly, he deliberately decided that he would give all his limited energy to the job to which he had been appointed, first Bursar then Senior Tutor of Jesus College, Cambridge. He never, in fact, wrote a book as such. All his books,

[1] For Manning's definition of Orthodox Dissent, and why he, a Congregationalist, chose to call himself an Orthodox Dissenter, see the Preface to *Essays in Orthodox Dissent*.

apart from professional contributions to volumes of history, are lectures or sermons later printed in book form. And thirdly and most important, he was not a popular speaker or writer. Not unpopular in the sense that people did not listen to him. On the contrary, such was the wittiness of his lectures that in Cambridge extra numbers attended a Society meeting if Manning was due to speak. But he was unpopular in the sense that he did not agree with most people in his generation either ecclesiastically or politically. He was a prophet, but not a popular prophet. He did not tell most people what they wanted to hear, and so he never became the popular writer whose books sold. Perhaps Manning was disappointed that the sales of his books were so small. He was a humble man, but he believed profoundly in the importance of what he had to say; there is an evangelical urge about all he wrote, and, although he never said so, one felt he was disappointed that so few seemed to listen. But he would never moderate the message to make it agreeable to the spirit of his age, to do such a thiug would never occur to him, which makes the message all the more useful for other generations. Manning wrote the truth as he believed it to be whether men liked it or not.

But the reasons he is unknown today can also be reasons why he should be known and listened to with increasing respect. He was an invalid. Often he received his students in his bedroom, sitting up in bed with his books around him. But he never complained about his infirmity and never in later years when attending residential conferences did he ask for any special arrangements to be made for his comfort. He never made people conscious that he was an invalid. But he had used his experience of ill health to give himself a meta—

rightful apprehension of the Christian Faith. His was a faith in no way based on youthful optimism or a belief in progress. Listen to what he had to say to the young Congregationalists of Durham and Northumberland at Easter, 1938.

'First, your individual hopes and beliefs will inevitably be damped down by the depression that comes from experience. I am sorry, but it is so. St. Paul says, I think, that experience worketh hope. It may—in the Church. But, in general, experience worketh mild despair. The world gets too much for you. What is worse, you get too much for yourself. You need to be able to fall back on a wider experience, a more deeply rooted hope than your own, and in the bad, bleak patches of life—believe one who has tried it—the Church can give you that wider experience and that deeper-rooted hope.

'And, second, as you get older the same thing happens. You can do an amazing lot while you are young, simply because you are young. You think today that you can do it because you have got hold of the right end of the stick, and that you will show the world a thing or two. It's great to feel like that; but it's because you are young, not because you have, in fact, got or can keep hold of the right end of the stick. As you get older and greyer and balder and bigger about the girth (if you are a man), or, (if you are a woman) as you take the necessary precautions to prevent any of these things from happening, you will feel that early fire die down. You cannot go by your own steam for ever. You will find a day when, if you are to keep going, you need the glow and the fire which the Church can give you . . . . . if you are not to settle down into a tiresome "stuck" sort of middle age, with all your early hopes and visions faded out.'[1]

Not for Manning 'a tiresome "stuck" sort of middle age.' But listen to some more of his words and remember the year was 1938.

'. . . . . the news of Jesus and the Resurrection is for you individually. It is for you A, B, or C, for you *here and now*, whatever happens to society and to Europe and to western civilization. The Good News can save the world, if it will hear, but, whether it will hear or not, the Good News can save you. St. Paul's writings made that clear. In his day the world in general was not going as he would have wished, as it is not going in our day as we could wish. But had St. Paul our dull, aching pessimism, that fear of things coming on the earth, that fainting of heart, as we wake, or just before we sleep? No: he fought bravely, cheerfully, confidently, through it all. "In all these things we are more than conquerors." "I am persuaded that neither life nor death"—you know the catalogue of all the things we fear—these cannot separate us from the love of God in Christ Jesus who died for us, nay rather, who is risen again.

'With the world in its present state, with our private lives overhung by our present terrors, the Church confidently brings us the news of Jesus and the Resurrection to do for us what it did for St. Paul. Now I want that done for me. I would count everything but dung to have it done for me.'[2]

Bernard Manning, like St. Paul, had had that done for him. He knew how to be more than conqueror. He had that gift this world can neither give nor take away. His writings today merit attention because it is the testimony of all who knew him; he lived by the

1 *Why Not Abandon the Church?* pp. 71–72.　　2 ibid p. 28.

Faith himself and radiated the hope of the Gospel to all who knew him.

Another reason he was not widely known was that he deliberately chose to live out his life in Cambridge. How faithfully and successfully he gave himself to his work there can be read in F. Brittain's memoirs of him, published by Heffer of Cambridge. That he should so choose can now be counted in his favour. The nearer one gets to some great men, the more the feet of clay are visible. In the case of Bernard Manning, it was those who knew him best who respected him the most. Read the testimony to him at the end of Brittain's book.

'When Bernard Manning died, requiems were said for him at Anglo-Catholic and Roman Catholic altars —a most striking tribute to the character of one who lived and died an uncompromising Dissenter and glorified in the name of Calvinist. It was as appropriate as it was spontaneous; for, although he was the peculiar glory of Congregationalism, he belonged to all who called themselves Christians. He did not belong entirely to his own or any other one century. He absorbed, as few or no others have done, the spirit of the Christian Church throughout the ages—of the early church and the medieval church no less than the fragmented Christianity of post-Reformation times. When he died, the Christian religion lost a great champion, capable of meeting any opponents on their own intellectual level. He championed the faith in season and out of season, in speech and in writing. He did this knowingly and he gloried in it. What he did not know was how greatly he championed the Christian religion by his daily life.'[1]

1 *Bernard Lord Manning: A Memoir*–Brittain. p. 90.

He gave himself to his work in Cambridge and all his books were talks written for particular audiences. How careful he could be, I have direct evidence. In the December of 1936 I asked him to give four talks on Congregationalism the following Easter. He replied he was honoured to have the invitation, but regretted that he did not know enough about the subject to write four talks in four months, but if I would repeat the invitation for Easter 1938, he would be honoured to accept. That from one of the world authorities on the subject: an illustration of his astonishing humility. His humility at times was, in fact, so astonishing that, when first experienced, one felt it must be assumed. But it was part of the man. One Sunday morning I went with Manning to the parish church, there being no dissenting chapel in the village, and at the church door stood aside to allow the older man and the man who had been my tutor to enter first. 'No,' said Manning, 'you go first. I should like to enter after an ordained minister of the Word.' And he meant it. As he said later to the young people at the conference—'If you are to get the preaching that you need, you must think highly, and you must teach your minister to think highly, of his sacred office.'[1] Dr Bett speaks of the same astonishing humility in his Preface to Manning's *The Hymns of Wesley and Watts*. 'I am also glad,' Dr Bett writes, 'that I saw him once, when I was on a visit to Cambridge . . . . . As one would expect, he was the most modest of men. Anyone might have thought on that occasion that it was he, and not I, who was having the privilege of meeting a man of genius.'[2]

1 *Why Not Abandon the Church?* p. 44.
2 *The Hymns of Wesley and Watts*, p. 5.

Manning always gave the other person the feeling that he mattered to him, and he was able to give that feeling because he really did. Some people to whom I have lent his books, who never knew the man, have deduced that he was cynical and abusive, a frightening, formidable person. Nothing could be further from the truth. He liked wit, to prick pomposity and to scoff at ignorance, but meet him and he was the kindliest and most humble of men. And he knew when to use his wit and when to refrain. In the discussion after one of his conference talks, he had failed to make his points with his characteristic wit, and I asked him to show some of the same spirit he showed in his evidence submitted to the Archbishops' Commission on the Relations between Church and State, 1931 (see *Essays in Orthodox Dissent*, p. 196 and following). 'No,' he said, 'the Archbishops' Commissioners were well able to look after themselves, but not these young folk.' But when later in the conference two budding scientific Ph.Ds. under-estimated him and decided to floor him in argument, the old light of battle came into his eyes and he was able magnificently and wittily to hold his own. But he hurt no feelings. He used all his considerable powers of wit and eloquence to defend truth and denounce error, never to hurt or to make another man feel small.

In the letter inviting Manning to the conference he had been asked to give four talks of about forty to forty-five minutes each. An example of his extreme care in preparation is that he wrote back asking if it should be forty or forty-five, he would like to know. He turned up to the conference with the four talks ready written—he read his material word for word, he had little gift for free speech. The first talk seemed just the right approach for the young people present, but Manning was not satisfied. 'I did not,' said Manning, 'get that quite right. I misjudged my audience. I know undergraduates and I know country folk, but I do not know young people from an industrial environment. I will rewrite my second talk this evening.' And so he did, foregoing any leisure time for himself. All the talks were rewritten in the light of what he learnt about the needs of the young people present through living with them and discussing with them. Those reading *Why Not Abandon the Church?* today may not realize how the talks were tailor-made to fit the audience of young people he was called on to address.

Manning's main concern was not to write something clever and witty in itself. His only concern, a true sign of humility, was to help the people he was speaking to. Good workmanship, he called it. I remember his advice 'Never say, "In the short time allotted to me." If it is impossible to cover the subject in the allowed time, then do not accept the invitation. If it is possible, then do not waste time talking about the short time allotted.' And he was particularly firm that a sermon or talk must be designed to help the people who were to hear it; no use to preach a sermon however brilliant to people who could not understand it or who did not need that particular sermon.

And the third reason, the most important, why Manning was not popular in his day was that he did not say the things that most people wanted to hear. With most people in his generation he just did not agree. As Brittain said, in the passage already quoted, 'He did not belong entirely to his own or any other one century.' In the Church, for example, he was highly critical of many of the leaders in his own

denomination, the Congregationalists, and had little
sympathy with many of the doctrines and customs
that his generation had inherited from Victorian
Congregationalism. And at the same time he had little
sympathy for the ways in which many wanted to
reform Congregationalism, and he could not agree
with so many of the arguments of the small, but kindly
and enthusiastic, band of men who worked for the
reunion of the Churches. In so many ways he was a
law unto himself. He was a devout and faithful Congregationalist, always present at Morning Worship at
Emmanuel, Cambridge in term-time, and at the
village chapel, often taking the services as a lay preacher
during vacations. He was intensely loyal to his own
denomination and always proud to bear the name of
Congregationalist. As his friend Brittain says on page
one of his memoirs—it is really the first thing to note
about his character—'The dominant feature of his
many-sided character was his unwavering loyalty.'
But he also loved the Book of Common Prayer and
attended Evensong in College Chapel every Sunday
in term, venerated the hymns of the Wesleys, and spoke
kindly words about the genuine devotion to be found
in any branch of the Church, including the Church of
Rome. Hear what he said to the Fifth International
Congregational Council at Bournemouth in 1930.

'We (Congregationalists) have no distinctive contribution to the literature of devotion or to the form and
manner of Divine Service. You will forgive a member
of Cranmer's College for saying that we have added to
the literature of devotion nothing comparable with
the *Book of Common Prayer;* and you will forgive a
Lincolnshire man for saying that we have added
nothing comparable with the *Hymns for the Use of*

People called Methodists. The most obvious characteristic of our worship is its variety; but even here we are
outdone. Even less uniformity than we can show has
been produced in Anglicanism by the Act of Uniformity.
The best traditions of our own worship we have yet to
recover from the Presbyterians. From them, more than
the Anglicans whom we are more inclined to copy,
we have much to learn. Our distinctive contribution
seems to me to concern none of these things. It concerns
churchmanship.'[1] Manning claimed the good in all
branches of the divided Church as his heritage and
respected them all. But this did not make him want
reunion at any price. As he said, 'I am afraid that
some sorts of reunion will only mean a new schism and
a harder task in future.'[2] Much of all he wrote was
on this subject of reunion, what Congregationalists
ought to believe and where they ought to stand, and
much of his most witty and effective writing was in
defence of dissent and against episcopacy. Let two
quotations speak for him now; the first from his
address to the Protestant Dissenting Deputies of the
Three Denominations in London, 1931.

'There is a present danger, an urgent danger, that
all that we of the three Dissenting Bodies have stood
for may be lost, because everyone nowadays wants
to be courteous and no one wants to be awkward. The
better our general relations with Anglicans are, the
more we must regret our ecclesiastical separation. It
would be so "nice" if we could all receive the sacrament
together, *so* "nice." Well, "niceness" is not a main
object of the Christian religion; and all this preaching
in one another's pulpits and occasional illicit inter-
communion, if it whets our appetites for the sweets of

1 *Essays in Orthodox Dissent*, p. 105. 2 *B. L. Manning*–Brittain, p. 76.

reunion *at any cost*, may betray that holy churchmanship which we received from our fathers. Episcopal ordination or confirmation may come to seem—to some of our ministers and laymen it has come to seem—a merely nominal price to pay for reunion, especially as so many Anglicans seem to attach no particular significance to episcopacy and those who talk most volubly about catholicity exercise private judgement and defy the bishops far worse than we do. Brethren, that way lies danger. Many Anglicans attach no meaning to episcopacy, because many Anglicans, like many Dissenters, are incapable of attaching any meaning to anything. But episcopacy has a meaning. In the Latin, the Greek, and the clearer-headed part of the Anglican Communion it has a very definite meaning with centuries of teaching and practice behind it. You cannot be rid of that meaning because it is convenient at the moment for a group of friends to forget it. To accept episcopacy at this stage of things, however "nice" a reunion we may get at the price, means that we unchurch the whole of the holy tradition which bred us and that we throw on a new and more virile race of Dissenters the onus of showing that in the dispensation of grace in the Church there is no circumcision and no uncircumcision, whether it be called episcopacy or by any other name.' [1]

And the second quotation is from an address to the Office Bearers' Association of the London Congregational Union in 1933.

'We want this union with all; but we do not want it at any price . . . . . We are saved by grace; by grace which comes as God's free gift, not in legally restricted channels controlled by attorneys in episcopal robes.

1 *Essays in Orthodox Dissent*, pp. 134–135.

And we are saved by God's full grace: not by some irregular, imperfect, diluted grace, just adequate to cope with the needs of mere Dissenters, but quite inferior to the 100 per cent streams, of which only the attorneys in episcopal robes can manipulate the sluice-gates. Against any such notion of the work of grace, we protest in season and out of season; and no prospect of union can silence our protest. It is the ancient battle fought by St. Paul against them of the circumcision which our fathers fought and which we fight. Is God's grace legally conditioned? Is episcopacy in the new dispensation what circumcision was in the old? Is episcopacy the essential channel for the full blessings of the new covenant in Christ as circumcision was the essential channel for the old covenant in Moses? My friends in the Anglican Body do not like me to ask that question in those terms, because, asked in those terms, it answers itself. But that—shall there be a new circumcision, a new legalism, under the Gospel?—*is* the issue between us and the episcopalians, Anglican, Greek or Roman.'[1]

The conclusion to which Manning came was—'If I am a member of the holy catholic Church of Christ, let me be treated as such frankly and openly: if they (the episcopalians) think I am not, let us pray God to show us who is wrong.'[2]

Manning's analysis of the ecclesiastical situation made him an unpopular thinker with most of his contemporaries. His analysis of the political situation made him no more popular. He could neither share the optimistic assessment made by so many churchmen in the 1920s and 1930s, nor agree with their way of tackling the political problems of his generation. In

[1] *Essays in Orthodox Dissent*, pp. 141–142.　　[2] ibid, p. 134.

his writings he continually rebuts what he believed to be the errors in analysis made by his fellow churchmen. Two quotations will illustrate the line of reasoning which appears continually in his writings. The first quotation is from this book.

'Religion on one side concerns itself with men. The historian can remind students of religion of certain features in human nature that they easily forget. Ill-founded optimism, the mother of despair, besets many people who study the development of religious opinion. They treat the subject simply as a clash of ideas and ideals. They assure themselves that if an opinion is true or good, it will survive and triumph. In the long run it may do so, but the historian notes that the run is sometimes very long indeed. There is an acute danger of underestimating the influence of force and civil government and unspiritual apparatus on religion. The machinery of civil society cannot fall into irreligious hands without the gravest consequences for religion. In the study of the decline of Christianity in the Near and Middle East, for example, too much attention has gone to demerits in the faith and practice of the Eastern Church, too little to the military situation, the proximity of deserts and steppes, the movement of peoples—forces over which moralists and bishops have no control.'[1]

Read also these words of his addressed to the Protestant Dissenting Deputies of the Three Denominations in 1931.

'There is abroad, especially among us Free Churchmen, a mischievous notion that truth cannot be suppressed, that good causes must flourish under persecution, that the blood of the martyrs is always the

1 *The Making of Modern English Religion*, pp. 114–5

seed of the Church. It may be true that in the long run, taking the world as whole, it is impossible ultimately to suppress truth. It may be true that under a little persecution badly applied the blood of martyrs may become the seed of the Church. But that is not a general rule. There are plenty of examples to the contrary. In Spain and Italy in the sixteenth century governments successfully framed public opinion in such a way as to crush Protestantism. In Russia today the Government has cut off the recruits to Christian population by its educational campaign; and it is producing a new generation as innocent of Christianity as eighteenth century Spain was of Protestantism. That these atrocious achievements may collapse centuries hence is no good reason for suffering them now if we can avoid it.' [1]

As Dissenters we may be particularly grateful to Manning because he makes us not only content in the tradition in which we were born, but proud of it. He showed us where we ought to stand and gave us a Dissent of which we could be proud. He fully admitted that Anglicanism had gained much by inheriting the 'going concern' from the medieval church, but showed also that they had paid too large a price for it—State Establishment. He taught us to respect and rejoice in and to claim for our own, as he did, all the good things which come to us from all branches of the divided Church, and yet at the same time to be loyal to and proud of that great truth enshrined in that tradition into which we had been born.

'Independency meant, no doubt,' Manning fully admitted it, 'some loss of venerable associations and sentimental appeal, but association and sentiment were

[1] *Essays in Orthodox Dissent*, p. 128.

an inconsiderable price to pay for a tremendous reassertion of the apostolic doctrine of the sovereignty of grace. This was the supreme achievement of Independency: to teach men to take off their shoes at the burning bush, not to botanize about it.' [1]

A second reason for thanksgiving, and one in which all Christians can share, is Manning's excellent book on Hymns. Few ever wrote better on the subject, and surely no one could write more entertainingly. He revealed the devotional and liturgical richness in a good hymn-book to people who had been singing hymns all their lives, and who had never really noticed the treasure which was theirs. No one who has read Manning can ever attend a service of worship at which hymns are sung without remembering something he had to say and being helped by it.

Another great service that Manning performed was his continual campaign against meaningless exaggeration. Hear, for example, these words of his—

'I wonder if you feel as I often feel when religious people talk, or, for that matter, when any sort of people talk, on public questions. They seem to me to exaggerate terribly. I have been told, off and on, by public speakers ever since the last war that unless I altered my ways of living I should bring another war on myself and on all Europe. Today I am told that I have done this, though I had been warned. Now it is no use exaggerating like that. We may be in for another war; I hope not, but, even if we are, I cannot honestly accuse myself personally of having done anything to bring it about, or of having neglected to do anything that would avert it. It would be mere hysterical

1 *Essays in Orthodox Dissent*, p. 162.

23

exaggeration to pretend that I have committed either fault.' [1]

Manning did what he could, refrained from doing what he ought not, but was completely free from that debilitating sense of guilt which comes from confessing sins for which there can be no pardon and release, because in the first place they were never committed. For the way in which Manning saved his followers from meaningless guilt, they will ever be grateful.

Manning championed the Faith by speech and writing in season and out of season, and he did so deliberately with a constant relish for a good fight. He was a magnificent apologist for the Faith, capable of taking on the best of its critics on equal terms. It gave those who knew him immense pleasure to have such a champion who was not in the least scared by any arguments his opponents used against him. But we had something better than Manning's arguments and that was Manning himself. He was a living disproof of the world's caricature of a Dissenting chapel-goer. He was not gloomy, he was happy; he was not ignorant, prejudiced, censorious and humourless, but a cultured man, with the widest interests, considerate, kindly and understanding of all human frailty, and with a constant supply of the most excellent humour. ' "By their fruits ye shall know them." I accept the challenge for the Churches with both hands and with all my heart.' [2] So Manning once wrote. His friends would certainly accept the challenge in Manning's case. The best of all Manning's brilliant arguments in defence of the Faith was himself.

Otterburn, Northumberland.   R. G. BELL

---

[1] *Why Not Abandon the Church?* p. 75.   [2] ibid, p. 20.

PREFACE

I N the summer of 1927 I was asked to try to show to
people who 'have no historical background whatever where the religious movements they see in the
world round about them today had their origin.' I
was to confine what I said as far as possible to England
and to the last four centuries. The people in view were
undergraduates reading natural science, mathematics,
languages and other subjects. Everyone knows in a
general way that the present comes out of the past,
but not everyone has the time or the inclination to
examine the past of the Churches for himself; and it
was for such people that I spoke. This book contains
the substance of the four lectures. It is published for
the same purpose as that for which the lectures were
given and for the same people. It is not a book for
students of history: they will find it full of flat truisms
and questionable generalizations.

The book frankly abandons chronology and makes
no attempt to be comprehensive. It does not pretend
to allot space in proportion to the importance of the
matters discussed. It omits some things quite as
important as those mentioned. It records a personal
impression, not an impersonal judgement. It contains
no catalogue of sects and parties.

No one can be impartial about the Christian religion.
I do not wish even to seem to claim the doubtful merit
of impartiality. My sincere admiration of almost
every religious movement discussed has, I hope,
prevented my writing anything that the people inside
any particular movement will feel unjust or unsym-
pathetic. If anyone does find anything of the kind I

apologize whole-heartedly in advance. That the lectures were tendentious I have not the slightest wish to deny or to conceal; but they were planned to illustrate the excellence of every historical presentation of the many-sided religion of Christ. The exaltation of all such presentations, not of some at the expense of others, was my aim.

The President of Cheshunt College, Cambridge, the Revd Dr Sydney Cave, has given me many valuable suggestions and much general help.

B.L.M.

Jesus College, Cambridge

INTRODUCTION

The Method of this Book

EVERYBODY knows something about the religious history of modern England, if only as a memory of history periods at school. Henry VIII and his divorce, 'bloody' Mary and her burnings, the Puritans and their odd objection to the ring in marriage, the quarrels of Archbishop Laud and the Presbyterians and the Independents, this and similar unpromising material we can all provide. For a full understanding of the position of religion in England today such things are of importance, but in a short book they can find no place. To try to work through the story chronologically would produce only the driest dead bones of an outline. To pass from sect to sect examining origins and peculiarities would produce something similar. Merely to mention things is of no value. It is better to omit many events and people and controversies, important as they may be, for the sake of giving at least a little life and meaning to some parts of the story.

The method of this book is then frankly to abandon any hope of bringing the whole pageant of English religious history since the Renaissance into a bird's-eye view. It will attempt something less ambitious. To pick out rather clearly three or four of the chief strands that have gone to make up the Englishman's religion and irreligion (for irreligion is an important side of the subject); to try to show what three or four of the principal religious parties and activities of our own time represent; from what places and persons, from what needs and experiences, they had their origin; and what 'contribution' they have made to our own environment and our own problems—this is the more modest method of the book.

Without some reference to church history no one can begin to understand the religious questions that are most debated today. What is meant by having some sorts of religion 'established' like Episcopacy in England and Presbyterianism in Scotland, and some 'free' or 'dissenting' or 'nonconformist' like Methodism and Congregationalism in both countries? How did Episcopacy, Presbyterianism, Methodism, and Congregationalism come to be in these positions? More important than such questions, perhaps, is this: how has it come about that whereas at the beginning of modern history four centuries ago church matters interested everyone however lewd or worldly or fashionable, today church matters tend to be the amiable, rather unexciting hobby of anaemic persons, decidedly not lewd nor worldly nor fashionable? Four hundred years ago it was of great consequence what a politician believed about purgatory and the nature of the consecrated elements in the Eucharist. Every man in the public eye, however scandalous a rascal he might be, professed much concern about religion. Today a politician may hold the highest offices without revealing what his religious interests are or if he has any. What does this change mean? Or again, if a man looks today at the division of Christians into sects and churches he may well inquire what vital force called these parties into being. The members of many of these parties seem very much like the members of the rest. Few could give any reasoned explanation of their adherence to this party rather than to that. What lies behind all these divisions? Even in religion there is no effect without a cause. Has the cause lost its power? Are these separate sects and parties mere survivals or is there a principle of life still in them?

To approach questions of this kind it is necessary, *first*, to see something of what modern English religion inherited from the Middle Ages four hundred years ago; and, *second*, to see what wasting destructive forces have been at work on that inheritance in modern times. This will include an examination of the so-called rationalistic criticism of religion which has helped to produce the great mass of irreligion in the world of today. This negative, destructive aspect of the changes being described in the first part of the book, the second part will concern itself with the positive, creative aspect: it will give an account of one or two of the principal new religious forces which have come into being in modern times, and it will trace the effect of them in English church life.

I

THE WASTING OF THE
MEDIEVAL LEGACY—INSTITUTIONS

WHAT did English religion at the beginning of modern history, about A.D.1500, inherit from the Middle Ages? In all ways of course we owe more to the Middle Ages than most people recognize. A useful, but far from comprehensive, account of our general debt appears in *The Legacy of the Middle Ages*.[1] The religious legacy can be divided into two parts: *first*, the doctrine and tradition, the non-material, spiritual side of the Church, and *second*, the institutional side, the Church regarded as a going concern, an instrument to perform certain functions in society; we need not for the moment define which particular functions they are. Modern England found in its hands ready for use, as part of the medieval legacy, this instrument with which something could be done. We will consider this first and the spiritual inheritance afterwards.

The Church as a going concern: words must not mislead us. The same words have at different times different meanings. *The Church* did not mean precisely the same thing in the Middle Ages as it means today. When people talk of the reduction of the power or influence of the Church in modern times it is important to remember that. What we call the Church is only a fragment of what medieval men called the Church; and very naturally a fragment, even if it is a large fragment,

---

[1] *The Legacy of the Middle Ages*, edited by C. G. Crump and E. F. Jacob, Oxford, at the Clarendon Press, 1926.

covers less ground, touches life at fewer points, and affects fewer people, than the whole did. Whether what we call the Church has less power and less influence than the corresponding fragment of what medieval men called the Church—there is the essential question. It is a question not easy to answer. It is indeed a question of which we may say, as admirable old Guillim said of a certain question in heraldry, 'it is a question of more difficulty to be resolved, than commodious if it were known.'

By the word Church medieval men meant something that modern men would call a second State. The Church of medieval men concerned itself, as our Church concerns itself, with doctrine, worship, and the application of Christian teaching to daily life; but it concerned itself also with many other things; or (if that expression be deemed inaccurate) it gave to doctrine, worship, and the application of Christian teaching to daily life a wider interpretation than we give. This had many consequences. Some of them we will observe.

Relatively many more people went 'into the Church,' that is, received Holy orders, than go into it today. What would seem to us a large proportion of the whole population of medieval England was in orders of some kind. Many men were in very low orders (below deacons' orders) with little intention or prospect of rising to the priesthood. These are to be thought of not as clergymen, but as *clerks* almost in the modern sense of that word.

Beside a great number of men an enormous amount of property (mainly land) belonged to the Church. But when the books say that at the end of the Middle Ages a fifth or a quarter or a third of all the land in

England belonged to the Church the statement, whether it is arithmetically correct or not, easily gives a very false impression. It is natural to assume that it means almost the same thing as if a fifth or a quarter or a third of all the land in England belonged to the Church today, that it was put by the Church then to the same sort of uses as it would be put by the Church today, and that it produced the same sort of effect on society generally. It is natural to assume this, but it is not entirely right to do so.

Church property was used in the later Middle Ages for purposes which today would not be recognized as church purposes. A great part of it was devoted to maintaining monasteries and monastic societies. And what were these? Certainly not all the people maintained by monastic property were living a life of prayer and contemplation and study. Many monastic societies consisted of a few monks in priests' orders and a vastly larger population of lay-men, servants and officials, whose ordinary day to day life did not differ very greatly from the life lived by the dependants of a great country house in the sixteenth, seventeenth and eighteenth centuries. The number of the true, professed monks for whose sake the whole system existed seems to have shrunk, as time passed, compared with the number of people living almost secular lives in attendance on them.

It is easy to exaggerate the religiousness of the Middle Ages because the medieval Church fills so much of the medieval scene, and we take it for granted that the Church was an exclusively religious institution. In any ordinary modern sense of the word 'religious' it was not. On one side it had its religious aspects and functions. But on another side it had this country

33

house aspect; on another a law courts aspect; on another again a diplomatic aspect. Hundreds of the clergy gave their time to studying and administering a law, the canon law; they spent their days in law courts and in the routine of legal business; but much of the business that came before those courts concerned matters to which at the present time no ordinary clergyman gives two minutes' thought in a day. It was not what we should call religious business.

Beside these agricultural and legal activities the Church at the end of the Middle Ages had diplomatic and even military activities. The Pope, it was said, drew from England in various sorts of taxation sums comparable with those that the king drew. The most interesting feature about papal taxation was, however, not its size but its object. In its object as well as in its size papal taxation was comparable with royal taxation. A great part of the revenue taken for the papacy, that is for the central organization of the Church in West Europe, went to maintain the diplomatic service and the foreign policy of the Roman court in Italy and Germany and elsewhere. Not infrequently a considerable part went to finance campaigns and to pay armies. We are not discussing whether the medieval or the modern interpretation of the functions of the Church is the better—each may be proper enough for its own circumstances—we are noticing some points in which the interpretations differed.

Now one of the things that happened in England at the time when modern history began was this: the secular state, represented by the King in Parliament (what we today call the State with a capital S), readjusted its relations with that second state that had hitherto existed alongside it, the medieval Church.

The medieval Church, for reasons which this book need not discuss, could not defend itself in England, and the functions which it had performed and the property which it had held in order to perform them were redistributed by Henry VIII, Edward VI, and Elizabeth. In brief, three things happened: the secularization of some of the functions hitherto performed by the Church, the destruction of others, and the control of the rest[1]—secularization, destruction, control.

First, the secular state took over for itself many of the functions and properties of the medieval Church. Things which the clergy, servants of the Church had done, laymen, servants of the State, now did.

In some matters the change was sudden; in some it was gradual. There are many illustrations. The king's courts had been trying for generations to steal business from the church courts, and after the changes of the sixteenth century they made rapid progress in reducing the sphere of the church courts to what would now be called strictly ecclesiastical business. Questions concerning wills and marriage, for instance, passed from church to secular jurisdiction. The consequence of such changes, though we take them for granted, has been enormous; for whereas almost every modern Englishman at some time in his life in some capacity appears before representatives of the Crown in a court of justice maintained by the secular State, hardly anyone today has experience of ecclesiastical courts. Many people do not know that they exist, and few laymen could mention any subject that comes within their jurisdiction. Yet the archdeacon and his

1 *Secularization* is used here to set State direction in contrast with ecclesiastical direction, not to set a materialistic outlook in contrast with a spiritual outlook.

court were once as familiar to the man in the street as the Justice of the Peace and the police court are today. A similar illustration of the passing of work from the Church to the State is in the relief of the poor. The modern poor law replaced medieval begging and medieval charity, the begging sanctioned and made more than respectable by the Church, the charity stimulated and organized by the Church. Men's whole attitude towards begging and beggars has altered; there is now a stigma on it that there used not to be when it was recognized by the Church and not frowned upon by the State. The education of children is another function of society that has passed for the most part from Church to State. Guilds and friendly societies for insurance and provident and social purposes of all kinds have become secular. These transfers and many like them have cut down very greatly the activities of the Church and multiplied the activities of the State. It is the modern process of secularization. Not only or chiefly property, but whole tracts of every man's life have passed from the supervision of the Church to the supervision of the State.

Beside secularization came destruction. The modern State put an end completely to some parts of the life of the medieval Church. Some of the institutions which had carried on church work it did not annex. It destroyed them. Of this destruction the outstanding illustration in England was the suppression of the monastic orders and the mendicant orders of friars. Everyone knows something about 'the dissolution of the monasteries,' but not everyone grasps the most important thing that it meant. It meant not only that a vast mass of buildings and property passed into the possession of the government or of private individuals; it meant too that many persons were forced out of one career into another, and that many who in the old order of things would have chosen a religious career now chose a secular career. One huge side of the medieval Church simply ceased to exist. A comparable change today—comparable in magnitude, obviously not comparable in results—would be the closing and destruction by the authority of the government of all churches and chapels where the congregations did not exceed, say, 100 persons, the transfer of the clergymen serving such churches and chapels to laymen's work, and the tolerance for the future of Sunday Schools only in the parishes affected. The disappearance of the monasteries, the monks, and the mendicant friars made a change in English religion hardly less sweeping. Almost half the people and the things that men had had in mind when they said the word *religion* suddenly vanished from their life. Apart from the rightness or the wrongness of what was done it is important to measure the magnitude of it.

The secular state did a third thing. Having secularized some functions of the Church and destroyed others, it set itself to control what remained. The State has had vastly more control over the Established Church since the Reformation than it had over the medieval Church. Two examples of this control will suffice. In modern times the secular government of the day has decided who shall be and (what is quite as important) who shall not be bishops. In medieval times the secular government of the day, though itself often very largely composed of clergymen, had not this undisputed control. It often tried to influence the choice of bishops; it often succeeded in making or ruining a career; but it was only one competitor among others for this influence, and the decisive voice was not then always the voice of the State. In modern times, too, the State has determined what forms of service shall be used, and what forms of service shall not be used, in parish churches. In the sixteenth and seventeenth centuries the State used this power freely and strongly, making frequent changes and ruthlessly expelling all clergymen who would not obey its liturgical instructions. In the eighteenth and nineteenth centuries State oversight in these matters has been less constant and State control less effective; but recent events have taught us that the State has not abandoned its claim nor permitted desuetude to annihilate it. To determine the forms of divine service is a power which the secular State did not take until the general exaltation of its authority over the Church at the beginning of modern history.

Secularization, destruction, control: these are key-words in any consideration of the fortunes of the Church as it emerged from the Middle Ages and came into relation with the modern State in the sixteenth century and onwards. Three types of building familiar to Englishmen visibly show forth the three processes. Many an Oxford or Cambridge College represents the secularization of part of the medieval inheritance: once a distinctly religious foundation planned mainly to train priests, it may have today no member of its society in Holy orders, very few ordinands among its undergraduates, its chapel almost deserted, its interests profane learning and sport. An abbey ruin represents the destruction of part of the medieval inheritance; and a parish church the state-controlled remnant that alone survived the coming of modern times. The change was not made all at once; but fast or slow it was made; and until it has been recognized no one can see English religious history squarely. In what ways these external changes affected thought will appear later.

If then we inquire what materials have gone to the making of the religious and the irreligious life of modern England, there appears first that part of medieval church institutions which survived the severe handling of the secular State. Crippled and truncated as this part was, the governments of Henry VIII, Edward VI, and Elizabeth granted it a continued existence under State control, and we may call it thenceforth the Established Church or the Establishment. Whatever may be thought of its claim to spiritual continuity with the medieval Church in England, it had at least continuity as a social organization and as a holder of property. In many ways, at least in the external life of men, it continued to fill the same place as the medieval Church had filled. We need some word to express this institutional continuity. We cannot speak of the medieval Church as 'established' and so make the connexion. We have therefore used the neutral expression 'the going concern' to describe that group of religious institutions which came out of medieval and persisted in modern life, and which makes the Established Church a representative of one side of the medieval Church. After every possible deduction from its resources has been fully allowed for, the going concern remained exceedingly influential.

What is true of England in this matter is true of all western Europe. The first element to be observed in the modern religious life of any country is that group of institutions built up by medieval Christendom and inherited by the modern world. Different countries have used it in modern times to teach very different doctrines. Some countries, Spain, for example, remained in communion with Rome and used the going concern to teach the new Romanism of the Council of Trent. In other countries it was used for other doctrines: in Sweden for Lutheranism, in Scotland for Calvinism. The point is that it continued to exist and to be used.

What precisely did this mean for the religious life of the English people? It meant that in England as elsewhere modern life began with numberless buildings, one at least in every village, devoted to religion, with religious associations and memories in everyone's mind. Many such buildings were being destroyed every day, and to that extent the impression on the popular mind was weakened. But after all the destruction of the sixteenth century a magnificent fragment of the medieval inheritance, the parish churches and the cathedrals, remained in continuous religious use. In addition to buildings the going concern included money: land, tithes, and endowments, making a large annual income and a vast capital sum. It was, to be sure, only a remnant of what once had been. An enormous proportion of the religious income and capital of medieval England (but it had been *religious* only in that wide sense in which we defined the medieval Church as religious) had found its way into the private pockets of the landed gentry and into the public coffers of the secular State.

More important than either buildings or money, as every cause and propaganda knows, are men. The going concern included some thousands of men devoted, like the buildings and the money, to religion. The sacred ministry as a whole-time vocation was a part of the medieval legacy. It was not inevitable that there should have been such a thing in the modern world. If this part of the medieval legacy—the clerical profession—had been destroyed, or were to be destroyed today, as some sentimentalists desire, to replace it would not be a quick or easy task. But it was not destroyed, and there were in hand when modern history began, ready for use, the bishops and the parish priests. These were but a fraction of the medieval personnel. All the rest were swept away. Many of the clerks of the medieval Church could indeed be swept away without affecting greatly what we should call the religion of the Englishman. When clerical lawyers and monastic landlords disappeared from society it affected his agriculture and the administration of his law but hardly his faith. The disappearance of the friars did affect the plain man's religion very considerably, for the friar had shared with the parish priest many of the everyday offices of every man's religion. The friar had no little share in promoting popular faith and spreading popular abuses. For good and for evil he had taken an active part in the people's life. But after these substantial deductions there was still a numerous body of men professionally concerned with the maintenance and spread of some sort of religion. It is easy for people in settled times to be too severe in judging them if in a time of unexampled mental turmoil they scarcely knew from year to year precisely what sort of religion it was.

The going concern had other aspects. It included as well as these tangible things, property and persons, others less definite but not less real. It included time. Modern Europe began with the clear opinion that a certain part of everyone's time was the property of religion exactly as the tithe, the church building, and the parson were. The amount and the reckoning of this religious time varied from country to country. In England the complicated medieval calculation of greater and lesser feasts, Sundays and saints' days, was simplified to a flat rate of one day in seven with a few of the greater feasts in addition. Religious time was not a matter of sentiment, of pious feeling, or of devoutness, but of plain fact. The farmer had to pay tithe whether he felt devoutly disposed or not; he might not use the parish church as a farm building (though he might so use the abbey) however conveniently placed for such a purpose the parish church might be; and similarly there was no legitimate positive use for a certain amount of time except religion. The time so reserved for religion was defined in different ways in different places, but the principle was universally recognized.

There was, too, prestige. Sadly as the secular State had shattered the prestige of the medieval Church much still remained. Two fundamental assumptions, which had been unchallenged and unbroken for ages, still held good: religion in some way concerned all men, and it was the business of the one Church to supply it—the business and the exclusive right. A last relic of this attitude shows itself even yet in the treatment of a recruit in the army. The two medieval assumptions appear. Every man has a religion: normally the Church of England, that which took over the going concern of the Middle Ages, represents it. In the absence of cause specially shown to the contrary that governs the situation. In every country in Europe when modern history began we find those same assumptions in favour of the going concern. Though it might change its creed and its rites many times, such changes did not invalidate the traditional assumptions in its favour. These held good despite everything for centuries. This prestige of religious institutions was, then, a part of the medieval legacy; and of all parts it was perhaps the most precious.

How has modern England treated what it inherited in all these ways from medieval Christendom? What is the position of the going concern today compared with its position in A.D. 1500?

In the first place it has survived. Every aspect of it that we have catalogued, and some that we have not, will be found to survive in the Established Church in England. Lapse of time, political and religious revolutions, have not broken this line of institutional connexion with the Church of the Middle Ages. Buildings, endowments, clergy, holy days, prestige— all survive. We are at present discussing tne Established Church only as a social institution, not as a vehicle of Divine grace. We may observe an institutionl connexion unbroken, without asserting or denying a continuity of ecclesiastical order or of episcopal succession in the ministry. Indeed the unbroken institutional connexion with the medieval Church which we have observed in the Established Church in England we may observe equally in the Established Church in Scotland, where no continuity of episcopal succession, but only of apostolical succession, is claimed; and in Sweden and in Spain, where claims differ from the claims in England.

But, in the second place, though surviving, all parts of the going concern have diminished in importance, some absolutely and all relatively. They play a steadily diminishing part in both public and private life.

Ecclesiastical buildings do not overshadow all others in the old way, and the newer the settlement the more inconspicuous they are. Everyone has noticed the contrast between churchless garden villages and the church-crowded centres of old cities. Even where ecclesiastical buildings are prominent not all belong to the Established Church. The problems of disendowment have almost ceased to interest anyone except the most intransigent Dissenters, because when it is compared with the growth of other capital and interest the wealth of the Established Church may be said to have dwindled into comparative insignificance. Its clergy have not multiplied with the population. Their numbers have begun to shrink not only relatively but absolutely. And for the life of the man in the street perhaps the most important diminution of the influence of the going concern in the last four hundred years is the loss of almost all sense of a religious claim on time. The disappearance of Sunday as a day on which the only legitimate positive employment was religious is the end of one of the great holds on the plain man which medieval bequeathed to modern Christianity.

It is important not to fog the main point by subsidiary discussions about the strict or loose observance of Sunday in the Middle Ages. It is indeed hardly to be questioned that the strict observance of Sunday which followed the Reformation in some countries would have delighted most medieval ecclesiastics. The Protestant reformers in that matter as in some others did only what medieval reformers had vainly desired to do. But the particular method of observance or the particular days to be observed might be changed, and indeed were changed, without any abandoning of the general principle that some periods of time had a

44

definitely religious connotation for all men. It was a claim to be respected, as ecclesiastical property was respected, regardless of the state of mind of any individual man. Until our own times this condition has held good. Men might respond or might not respond to that for which the holy day stood; but when the holy day came round they could no more avoid the reminder of religion than when they passed a church which perhaps they never entered. No longer is this true of many sections of society. A generation is arising for whom the first and most inevitable connotation of what used to be a religious day will be golf or tennis, char-à-banc or cinema according to season or social class.

We can measure this same loss of influence on another and a quite different line. We can watch the transformation of the medieval Church-State into the modern secular State, a society which was as much concerned with the religious as with the temporal affairs of men into a society which, as far as it can, purposely excludes all religious affairs from its consideration. This process began with toleration. It ends in secularization. Let us examine the transformation briefly.

For many generations after the beginning of modern history the going concern held the field. It had always held the field: men assumed that it always would do so. When new religious forces appeared their one policy and first ambition was to capture the Church established by law, to harness, and to control it. By that method alone could they make themselves felt. There arose, therefore, only one question: in what ecclesiastical interest, Roman, Lutheran, or Calvinist, would the Established Church hold the field? It did not at first occur to anyone that the field might be divided, and that the religious life of England could be or ought to be affected seriously by anything but the one Established Church.

But one of the key-words to the situation at the beginning of modern history was *control*, control by the secular State. The going concern had become a Church now definitely established by secular law and was more than ever closely connected with the State. Any attempt to capture and influence it in this or that religious interest inevitably brought a political struggle in the State. And so it fell out in English history in the seventeenth century. Some time elapsed before the competing religious forces generated in the Reformation period were articulated and differentiated, but when the confusion of religious thought and aspiration had crystallized into clear-cut parties, Laudian, Presbyterian, Independent, there began the final struggle to get a grip on the Established Church. The effort of these competing schools of religious thought to control its machinery brought about the political-ecclesiastical struggle called the Civil War. Looked at from a religious point of view, that war was a struggle of the several parties that had emerged from Reformation thought to capture the valuable relics of the legacy of the Middle Ages. Each party saw that if it was to capture these relics it must first capture the secular government which now controlled them.

The result of the seventeenth century struggle was what no one had sought. No party had proved strong enough to get all that it wanted, whilst only the Roman Catholics, Unitarians, and agnostics had been too weak to get anything that they wanted. The issue, briefly described, was this: the episcopalian party kept control of the Established Church, but in order to compensate the parties that had not got control of it its position was still further weakened—the first weakening we have observed under Henry VIII, Edward VI, and Elizabeth—by the device of toleration. The stronger and more respectable of the defeated parties, abandoning now all hope of controlling the Established Church, were for the first time permitted to exist cheek by jowl with it—the Presbyterians, the Independents, the Baptists and the Quakers (who rather later secured exceptionally good terms for themselves).[1] Existing cheek by jowl with theEstablished Church did not indeed mean a full share in the life of the nation for these parties. They had not full, nor nearly full, rights of citizenship; but if they cared to forgo political existence the State suffered them to have religious existence. This made an enormous change in the medieval inheritance. Room had been found in society for more religion than the going concern. Such was the eighteenth century situation.

It was a peculiarly English solution of the problem. It did not destroy the rights of the Established Church. In theory it hardly curtailed them. The secular State did not renounce its control over religion. It did not proclaim general toleration. But specified bodies of Christians on specified terms were allowed to exist beside the controlled and privileged body. In the words of the Toleration Act itself certain of Their Majesties' Protestant subjects, differing from the Church of England, were exempted from the penalties of certain laws.

But, however carefully Parliament covered it, a breach had been made in the Established Church. It was sure to be widened. The widening was the work of

1 Quakers were allowed to celebrate marriage according to their own rites long before the other Dissenters had this liberty.

the late eighteenth century and the nineteenth century. By the end of the nineteenth century England had, instead of a State which grudgingly granted limited toleration as an exception, an almost completely secularized State. Toleration had become exceedingly wide. It had come to include Roman Catholics, Unitarians, Jews, and agnostics. Toleration was indeed no longer a correct term, for people outside the Establishment had not only religious freedom but almost complete rights of citizenship.

How had these changes since the Civil War affected the Established Church? Very seriously. The industrial revolution with its great accumulation of new capital had reduced the financial importance of the Established Church in society. The extension of toleration to the point of almost completely secularizing the State had reduced its legal privileges. A citizen could now live the full life of an Englishman without touching the going concern at any point or permitting it to touch him. This state of things would have been inconceivable in A.D.1500. The Established Church still has a certain, but a diminishing, social prestige. What was once the unique going concern has almost become, from the legal point of view, one sect among the rest.

To clear-sighted men in the Established Church a hundred years ago it was already plain that this was happening. The political foundations inherited from medieval Christendom and laid afresh in the Reformation settlement were failing. They would fail more and more. What would happen when they had utterly failed? The state of its political foundations made the Established Church inquire where its spiritual foundations were laid. The result of this inquiry was the Oxford Movement.

II

THE WASTING OF THE
MEDIEVAL LEGACY—BELIEFS

L ET us return to the questions with which we began. Why, when modern history begins, has everyone, however lewd or worldly or fashionable, some concern about Church matters? Why after four hundred years do Church matters concern only comparatively few people? A part of the answer has already appeared. There used to be many reasons beside religious reasons for taking an interest in the Church: today there are hardly any. So much have four centuries done.

That makes but one side of the story. We have looked only at forms and institutions. We have left greater matters unregarded. At the risk of a certain unnaturalness and unreality we thought first of the Church merely as a going concern with property and officials and status. We did not inquire what it was doing through the four centuries of modern history, but only what was its equipment when it started and how much of that it had lost on its way.

We pass to more fundamental inquiries. The legacy of medieval Christendom to the modern world was not only an institution which governments and politicians might attack. That legacy has suffered attacks too from more subtle foes. The four centuries of modern history might have robbed the Church of almost all the political, financial, and social influence that once gave it power among men, but if its religious claim on their allegiance had remained unimpaired the Church might smile at the loss of its adventitious attractions. It might even condemn them as meretricious. But have not the four centuries of modern history also reduced its religious hold on men? Has there not been an intellectual and spiritual wasting away of the medieval inheritance?

The positive name commonly given to this intellectual and spiritual wasting away of the medieval inheritance is the growth of rationalistic criticism. Rationalistic criticism, the books say, has reduced the hold of the Church and of Christianity on the mass of men and is still reducing it. Rationalistic criticism is a general name convenient enough for our use, if it is used with some precautions. The word rationalistic is understood to be in inverted commas. We do not propose to beg the question in advance. Rationalistic criticism is to be accepted as rationalistic only in the same provisional and conventional sense as free thought or free churchmanship is free, Anglo-Catholicism, English and catholic, and modernism modern. Rationalism is a name only. To use it does not bind us to the opinion that rationalism is truly more reasonable than any other view of the universe. It may be; it may not be; that is not the historian's affair. He must take words as he finds them in common use. Unlike Humpty-Dumpty he cannot make them mean what he thinks they ought to mean.

Another precaution must be taken. It is necessary to set it out at some length unless the whole process of rationalistic criticism of medieval assumptions is to be misunderstood—as usually happens. It would be an error to suppose that, because men speak of rationalism as a feature of the last four centuries, there was little or no reasoning in the Middle Ages. At no time in the history of thought before or since did logic and the science of reasoning stand so high as then. Reasoning was the very foundation of medieval education; all examining took the form of a contest in rational argument. The Middle Ages had too much, not too little, reasoning; but in the Middle Ages all the reasoning went on inside the four corners of the Christian faith. The premises were all Christian; not, as the ignorant maligner of the medieval Church stridently asserts everywhere, because the clergy stifled all independent effort to think, but for the entirely adequate reason that when the Christian faith contained almost all the materials available for reasoning about, it was impossible to reason very far outside it. Now the medieval churchman found himself very nearly in this position. His historical knowledge did not range beyond Christendom and the Near East and arranged itself easily according to the scheme of human development sketched in the Bible. He had no difficulty in writing a short history of mankind from the Creation to his own day. Every monastic chronicler did that. And if history lay snugly within the faith, natural science had hardly begun to raise awkward problems outside it. Such knowledge of natural science as the medieval churchman possessed did not provide many obstacles. It is indeed notorious that the Middle Ages did not make great progress in natural science. The medieval churchman, therefore, had no need to go through an intricate series of mental gymnastics to reconcile his faith with the rest of his knowledge, nor at the command of his Church did he close his eyes to knowledge staring him in the face. Those practices are modern, not medieval.

It is not sufficient merely to state that the Middle Ages did not feel certain religious difficulties felt in modern times. If we are to understand their importance to later generations we must inquire a little more particularly why they appeared so late. Medieval men did not face certain problems, because they had not pursued certain lines of historical and scientific thought. It is often suggested that they did not pursue those lines of thought because they were preternaturally stupid or because they were under the spell of sinister obscurantist influences. To advance explanations of that kind is to declare a bankruptcy in historical thinking. Medieval men gave less thought to history and science than we give because they had more urgent work in hand.

What was this work? People easily overlook the essential character of the Middle Ages. They speak of them as the ages of faith or the dark ages; they call them romantic, beautiful, horrible, priest-ridden, and almost everything else. They do not notice that before and behind all else the Middle Ages were, in Miss Rose Macaulay's phrase, 'dangerous ages.' The Middle Ages, the thousand years between the collapse of the Roman Empire and the Renaissance, lie between two periods when the characteristic civilization of Europe was much safer. That ancient world, when Greek and Latin culture dominated the Mediterranean lands, had barbarian neighbours who did not share its religion or its civilization; and in the last four centuries Europe has had such neighbours. But for many centuries the ancient world was comparatively safe from external interference as modern Europe has been safe. Each could live its own life in its own way and hold its enemies in check. Each had material and financial and military supremacy.

Now the essential character of the Middle Ages is that these things were not true of them. Medieval Europe had not the same sort of material and military predominance over its neighbours. It was not even secure. There was danger of every sort, pressing and hardly to be evaded. Above all there was the supreme danger that the whole fabric of western civilization, founded on the culture of the Roman Empire and the Christian faith, would go down before races which shared neither, which either were barbarians or had an irreconcilable civilization and an irreconcilable religion. For a thousand years Christendom lived in a state of siege, suffering incursions and invasions from every quarter: from Arabia, from Central Asia, from Scandinavia, from the north European plain. The year A.D.1000 saw the situation almost at its worst. Only two fragments had escaped the most disastrous results: Asia Minor with part of the Balkan Peninsula (which was itself to suffer indescribable things later), and North Italy, France, and the Rhineland. Every other region of the Christian Roman world had suffered conquest by pagans or infidels.

From A.D.1000 to A.D.1500 came the beginnings of the recovery which is still going on. This has given back to Europe gradually the political control of all the lands of the Roman Empire except Asia Minor, and has restored Christianity too in most of them.

Such, then, was the position of the men of the Middle Ages. They stood in great peril between two comparatively safe epochs, the ancient classical world of Greece and Rome and the spacious opulence of modern times.

Without this background of the condition of medieval

life no one can begin to understand the alterations in thought that occurred four hundred years ago. Many histories of the development of political and natural science illustrate this. It would be idle of course to pretend that there is not a vast difference between medieval and modern ways of thinking about many subjects; but it is merely silly to call medieval thinking cramped, superstitious, priest-ridden, warped by Biblical notions, and such like. We must appreciate the conditions in which the thinking went on. Natural science, literary and historical criticism, intellectual life of any kind is very good, but when all is said it is a luxury. It is the sign of a safe and leisured society that is quite sure of its bread and butter for today and tomorrow at least. Medieval Christendom in the main, and for most of the time, was not such a society, and it could not afford such luxury. Its chief concern was to keep body and soul together. The most it could hope to do in many places and periods was to preserve as much as possible of the intellectual inheritance that had come down from more happily placed antiquity. 'Gather up the fragments that nothing be lost' is the keyword of much medieval scholarship. It explains the jumbled encyclopaedic scrap-books of writers like St. Isidore of Seville, who were more anxious to preserve than to understand the results of earlier thought. To preserve was indeed then the most urgent duty of society. It was not romanticism that gave medieval thought its backward look. It was not obscurantism. It was common sense.

If the danger should pass or be reduced, reaction was sure to follow. The thought dominant in the period of danger was sure to be criticized for the harsh conservative forms which had then been necessary. Now it happened that the thought in possession of men's minds in the Middle Ages was Christian thought. It might not have been so. Had the Roman Empire fallen before it had been converted, the great movement of new thought at the end of the centuries of medieval peril would have been critical, not of a rather stereotyped Christianity, but of some non-Christian line of thought. Whatever had been in possession of men's minds during the thousand years of siege was bound to be attacked when the siege was over. Christianity was in possession and it felt the attack; but it was attacked because it had been in possession, not because it was Christianity.

Having taken these precautions, we may now examine the wasting away of the spiritual side of the medieval legacy. In the last four centuries a great part of modern life has come outside the religious framework that formerly enclosed it. Rationalistic criticism has secularized much thought as the State has secularized many institutions.

The first great landmark in the history of rationalistic criticism of the Christian view of life is the Renaissance. By the Renaissance West Europe recaptured knowledge of the world that lay behind the strenuous, dangerous Middle Ages, that old and opulent and comparatively safe world of the Greek City State and the Roman Republic and Empire. The recapture was made through literature. For the first time for centuries, the west read the whole of extant Greek literature and parts of Latin literature long neglected. Greece, its life and thought—this was the main discovery; and as part of the discovery of Greece there was the Greek New Testament, the key to any study of Christian origins.

But in what sense is it true that these discoveries were the origin of modern rationalistic criticism of Christianity? We need to be exceedingly cautious. People often talk as if the Renaissance by some mystic process of enlightenment gave men a new sense, a sense of truth which unfitted them to rest longer in ecclesiastical fables and fictions. People talk of the Renaissance as the beginning (or the beginning again after a lapse of ages) of a search for truth in a scientific spirit, the beginning of a scientific examination of historical documents. They seem to make out that some new object 'truth,' or some new method 'scientific,' had burnt into men's minds and altered all their procedure. It is a solemn and pleasing duty to warn ourselves against such fantasy. If the scholastic philosophers of the Middle Ages were not seeking for truth no one knows what they were doing, and words have no meaning. And what is meant by any new 'scientific' method of examining historical documents? To examine historical documents in a 'scientific' manner means neither more nor less than to examine them honestly, sincerely, fearlessly, with all the knowledge of your time at your disposal. Honesty, sincerity, fearlessness, and power to use all the knowledge of one's time did not come into the world at the Renaissance. The scholars of the Middle Ages were not unfamiliar with this method nor unpractised in it. The knowledge at their disposal was amazingly less than the knowledge at the disposal of the scholars of the Renaissance, and in consequence their judgements diverged more from our own; but that is all. There was at the Renaissance no break in the method or the object of the search for truth—that perennial search— there was only a sudden vast increase of knowledge.

Men were not endowed with some new point of view or some new mental process, which put the traditional Christian point of view out of count. Yet that is a common enough perversion of what happened at the Renaissance, and it is assumed that until our own times only a few people had wit or honesty enough to admit that this had happened.

What did happen? Laying aside theories of a semi-mystical rationalistic illumination, we may discern two main effects of the work of Renaissance scholars upon Christian beliefs, especially in England.

First, many men's confidence in the Church as the holder of Divine truth suffered a shock when they perceived for the first time how far it had moved from its origins. The Renaissance scholars had increased knowledge of the past at their disposal. They proved that some of the documents on which the Church founded its claims to some of its powers and functions as a social institution were forgeries, or at least were not as old as had been supposed. The Popes claimed temporal power in Rome to rule it as kings, and a main support of this claim was a document called the Donation of Constantine. People in the Middle Ages believed that Constantine, the first Christian Roman Emperor, had given the right to rule Rome, Italy, and all the west to the bishop of Rome, Sylvester, and had removed his own capital to Constantinople in order to give the bishop a freer hand. A Renaissance scholar, Laurentius Valla, in the light of the new knowledge of literature proved that the document was written centuries later than Constantine's lifetime, and that if the temporal power of the Pope rested on it it rested on a myth. In early days the Pope had had no such power. Here was a wide divergence from origins.

An increased knowledge of the Bible revealed other examples of divergence. Repentance, when men looked at the word in the Greek New Testament, was seen to mean a change of mind, not the doing of penance. They learnt to contrast our Lord riding on an ass in humble triumph and the Pope borne in state procession on men's shoulders, our Lord washing the disciples' feet and men kissing the Pope's toe.

These things were but a beginning, and the most important results were indirect. People were not shocked into agnosticism by the discovery that a few falsehoods had been told in the interests of the Church or a few false documents palmed off in an uncritical age; but they came very gradually to realize that an historical evolution had gone on. A very elaborate ecclesiastical system had developed from simple beginnings. This made them view the Church and its teaching in a new light.

There was, it seemed, no such absolute authority for what the Church taught as had been believed. Its authority had grown. It had not always grown: sometimes it had been constructed by statesmanlike rulers. One could not assume that the Saviour himself actually commanded all that the Church now commanded. Some divergence was proved. More was likely to be proved. It made the public mind uncertain, unconfident.

The effects of this literary criticism continued to work in later centuries. For a time after the Renaissance some people believed that they had solved their difficulty by appealing to an infallible book. The Bible, which had provided such effective criticism of the infallible Church, they took for an accurate, unadulterated account of revealed religion. It at least might stand as authoritative. But soon the same historical criticism which had tested the infallible Church of the Middle Ages by its own documents tested the infallible book by itself. It showed that the book itself was a product of history. Like the divine society the Bible had been subject to the laws of historical evolution. The Bible therefore seemed to suffer from the very same deplorable uncertainty in authority which had been discovered in the Church and in Christian tradition.

The second effect of the Renaissance that we must notice was not less far-reaching. The Renaissance gave back to men what they had long lost: intimate knowledge of the world of Greece and Rome. The study of pagan letters revealed the richness, the fullness, the colour, the joy that life might have had, indeed had, without Christianity. It all came back. Those who are familiar with classical literature can picture for themselves as these men first saw it that confident, brilliant, bold-eyed, lustful life; the unsophisticated pagan virtues in their splendid simplicity, 'to ride, to shoot, and to tell the truth'; 'the glory that was Greece and the grandeur that was Rome.' Those who do not know the sources may find in English versions of Horace or of *The Greek Anthology*[1] the pathos and the laughter of that old ruined world. But the first vivid impression that its grace made on the men of the Renaissance none of us can ever fully feel again. We lack the background on which they saw this pagan pageant: the background of the dangerous Middle Ages, ages as they saw them not of painted glass and Morris fabrics, but of turmoil and darkness and risk for the very elements of a struggling civilization. So

1 Walter Leaf, *Little Poems from the Greek*, or A. C. Benson, *The Reed of Pan.*

seen the Christian ages, the years of salvation, poor, turbulent, squalid, and ill-bred, made an unpleasing contrast with the urbane serenity of the antique scene, the civilization of Greece and Rome in its prime. The Gospel, it seemed, was not quite all that men had supposed, not so utterly necessary to possess nor so utterly satisfying when possessed, if life without it had once been as good as ancient literature made it appear. After what men had now seen the Gospel could not again fill quite as much of their mental horizon. The story goes of a certain cardinal that he would not read the epistles of St. Paul for fear of spoiling his literary style. He was but a type of many in that generation who forsook the Apostle and the Apostle's Master, having loved this present world, for this present world was seen by the new humanism as medieval Christendom had never seen it.

After four hundred years for reflection on these matters the man of the present day may interpolate that for the scholars of the Renaissance their little learning was a rather delusive thing. A very little more of their own historical criticism would have led those naïve admirers of Greece and Rome to observe that those same ancient civilizations, satisfying as they looked, had found themselves so unsatisfying as to accept the very Gospel now disparaged for their sake. The issue of *The Greek Anthology* was, historically, the New Testament—if we may let those books stand as symbols for pagan life and Christ's religion. It is at least flying in the face of history to wish to replace the New Testament by *The Greek Anthology*. The Renaissance in due time was to find for itself the truth of the bitter words:

On that hard pagan world disgust
And secret loathing fell;
Deep weariness and sated lust
Made human life a hell.

But for the moment that was not clear.

The second great landmark in the development of rationalistic criticism is the seventeenth century, taken as a symbol of a great movement of thought. The seventeenth century is only a symbol. Much of the most important part of the movement lies outside it. Here was no such compact kind of discovery as in the Renaissance, but in more gradual ways as the result of many men's work in many generations a new world, comparable with the new world of old Greece, came into view, the world of Nature, spelt with a capital N. The study of Nature claimed more and more attention. The second landmark was what is called the beginning of the modern study of the natural sciences.

The work of Galileo in astronomy put our planet, and ourselves with it, in a much more insignificant place in 'the scheme of things entire' than we had been wont to assume. A similar result followed more careful study of what was on and in the planet itself, the world of animals and plants and rocks. Astronomy had altered the setting of our world among the worlds. Geology and biology altered the setting of man in our world. The same conclusion came on many lines of thought. The universe appeared bigger, older, more complex, less comprehensible than before. Divisions became less cut and dried; and as the work begun by Bacon and others in the seventeenth century was continued in the eighteenth and nineteenth centuries, and the great evolutionary process became in its main outlines apparently clearer, the old certainties about life began to waver a little. Immeasurable spaces, vast epochs of time, untold relationships of man with the animal creation, all appeared. It was confusing. A man could not now pass with comfortable chronology from the Creation to the year in which he was writing, as the monastic chroniclers had done. Not only was it more difficult to see what had happened; it was almost impossible to see what would happen or what was intended to happen. Men found it less easy to be sure about what the Creator had in mind at the Creation than they had once done. Milton, living near the beginning of the movement, had found it difficult to

> . . . *assert Eternal Providence,*
> *And justify the ways of God to men.*

Few since his day would be rash enough to attempt it in the old manner.

There is in William James's *Human Immortality* a passage which describes the new situation with a certain grim humour.

'For our ancestors the world was a small, and—compared with our modern sense of it—a comparatively snug affair. Six thousand years at most it had lasted. In its history a few particular human heroes—kings, ecclesiarchs, and saints—stood forth very prominent, over-shadowing the imagination with their claims and merits, so that not only they, but all who were associated familiarly with them, shone with a glamour which even the Almighty, it was supposed, must recognize and respect. These prominent personages and their associates were the nucleus of the immortal group; the minor heroes and saints of minor sects came next, and people without distinction formed a sort of background and filling in. The whole scene of eternity (so far, at least, as heaven and not the nether place

62

was concerned in it) never struck to the believer's fancy as an overwhelmingly large or inconveniently crowded stage. One might call this an aristocratic view of immortality; the immortals—I speak of heaven exclusively, for an immortality of torment need not now concern us—were always an *élite*, a select and manageable number.

'But, with our own generation, an entirely new quantitative imagination has swept over our western world. The theory of evolution now requires us to suppose a far vaster scale of times, spaces, and numbers than our forefathers ever dreamed the cosmic process to involve. Human history grows continuously out of animal history, and goes back possibly even to the tertiary epoch. . . . Bone of our bone, and flesh of our flesh, are these half-brutish pre-historic brothers. Girded about with the immense darkness of this mysterious universe even as we are, they were born and died, suffered and struggled.'[1]

The general effect was not unlike the effect produced at the Renaissance when men discovered how full and how cultivated pagan society had been. The discoveries of natural science seemed to raise the same question. Was there not more in human life than the Gospel had taken into account? New facts had now come into prominence, facts outside that scheme of Christ's religion which once had seemed to cover the whole ground. Was the Gospel utterly adequate? Was the Gospel utterly necessary? These developments and these inquiries are still with us.

The eighteenth and nineteenth centuries have produced a third line of criticism: not literary as the first was, nor scientific as the second, but rather

1 Page 62 *et seq.*

human or social. It is difficult to find a label.

These two centuries have made the industrial revolution, and have suffered from it. Its appalling social results brought home first to Christian consciences and later to others the responsibility that all men have for seeing that other people get at least a chance of making something tolerable of their lives. That is an ambition modest enough, but everyone knows how deplorably short of attaining even that ambition industrial England fell in the nineteenth century and still in some ways and some places falls.

The period of the industrial revolution made in the outward manner of English life changes more speedy and more astonishing than any that an equal length of time had ever made before. These very changes, in their rapidity and the possibilities that they opened, drew men's attention to the opportunities and successes, the injustices and failures of human life. Every man, people reasoned, had but a limited number of years to pass upon this earth, it might be twenty, it might be a hundred. Spring, summer, autumn, and winter for a strictly defined period, he was to see day come and night follow. That at least was certain, though most other things were doubtful. But it was also certain that millions did not spend this life, the only one of which they could be sure, in a full or happy or even decent way. The tragic and unnecessary waste of man's passing years called for action. It induced people to give more and more attention to the problems of this mortal life. There is no wealth but life, they cried, and they do not deserve overmuch blame if for the moment they forgot that life means more than life of the body. The wrongs calling for redress in this world made other-worldliness almost a crime. The humanitarians of the eighteenth and nineteenth centuries were no doubt in many ways quite absurd people. The Labour Party of the twentieth century is no doubt in many ways as short-sighted an affair as ever crossed the human stage. But when all is said the humanitarians and the Labour Party grasped one truth: there is need (whatever else may be needed also) to see that poor human bodies shall eat and drink and sleep and work in a minimum of comfort and decency.

What has this to do with rationalistic criticism of Christianity? It sounds a far cry, but it is less far than it sounds. Like the Renaissance and the study of the physical universe, this more careful examination of the human scene, forced by the melodramatic horrors of industrialism, has revealed a new set of facts: the actual situation of millions of men. Yet this particular set of facts, the realities of the human situation, was the very thing which religion had claimed as its own province and the raw material of its work. It might have been no serious reproach against religion that it had underestimated the niceties of pagan culture or miscalculated the dimensions of the universe, but living needy men and women and children—these were the sheep that it had set out to tend. Whatever its other negligences and ignorances, the Church had claimed at least to understand the cure of human souls. Its own province it seemed to have neglected. Its own problem it seemed to have failed to realize and even to have mis-handled when, as an institution, it had come up against the political aspirations of the masses. The conservatism of the Church, its slowness, its ungenerous response to appeals from the victims of modern industrialism, its failure to be in the van of progressive movements: malice has exaggerated these things monstrously; but there was something for malice to exaggerate. It is exaggeration: it is not the sheer invention of a charge.

This side of modern life, the struggle for social justice, has secured, and is securing, more of everyone's attention. Concern about the improvement of material conditions, unlike the discoveries of the Renaissance and of natural science, has touched not the learned few but the unlearned many; but, like those discoveries, this concern has served to diminish the importance of religion in the eyes of many men and to shake their confidence in it. It has provided a rival with claims on their conscience, as ancient Greece provided a rival for their admiration, and natural science a rival for their contemplation. Religion has suffered severe competition in artistic, intellectual, and moral spheres: that is one catchword in which we can sum up the effects of the Renaissance, the new study of natural science, and the movement for social justice. They all come into line. They have developed other interests for men. They have shaken men's belief first in the importance of what religion stands for, and then even in its adequacy to deal with the problems that it has chosen as peculiarly its own.

III

MARTIN LUTHER
AND THE REDISCOVERY OF
EVANGELICAL RELIGION

THE centuries of modern history have wasted and
destroyed much of the medieval inheritance;
but modern history is not merely a tale of the destruction of religion. Creative forces have been at work.
New institutions have arisen to replace the old. New
springs of piety have been opened; or rather the old
springs have been approached by new direct ways that
in a thousand years most men had forgotten. We shall
not attempt to describe one by one all new contributions
to Christian thought and practice. We shall discuss
two of the greatest of the new positive forces generated
by religion in modern times. We shall follow them down
the centuries, and as they will pass by a number of
churches, sects, parties, and movements, we shall see
something of these on the way. Our aim will be to
perceive the value of these two streams of religious
thought rather than to give an account of the several
religious denominations that each has inspired.

In the search for new forces in English religion
national sentiment might direct us to our great country-
man John Wyclif, 'the morning star of the Reformation.'
But national sentiment would misdirect us. We need not
underestimate the effect of Wyclif's work—we are not
yet in a position to make an estimate of it—but we
cannot find in him the origin of a new refreshing force
for English religion. As a critic of abuses Wyclif was

formidable. As a preacher of righteousness he was admirable. As a prophet of future relations of Church and State he was accurate. In his work for the translation of the Bible into English he showed a trustworthy instinct for what was to be decisive in the campaign against the medieval Church; and so far he did constructive work. But the most part of his work was negative and critical, a protest against other men's errors rather than a new exploration for himself of the riches of Christ's religion or a new presentation of them to others. John Milton suggested that only the 'obstinate perverseness of our prelates' prevented Wyclif from making the work of Luther and Calvin unnecessary and their names unknown; but for the suppression of Wyclif 'the glory of reforming all our neighbours had been completely ours.' Melanchthon judged otherwise. Though he found that Wyclif had anticipated the Reformers in some ways, he did not find that he had the root of the matter in him. When we have seen what seemed to the Reformers the root of the matter, the positive contribution to religion that they had to bring and how that outweighed all amendment of manners and redress of abuses, we shall be disposed to agree with Melanchthon and not with Milton.

We must begin with Luther, not with Wyclif. Now we may admit at once that Luther has had in recent years a somewhat undesirable reputation. He has been made responsible for the destruction of many works of art that accompanied the Reformation, and since art has for many men more value than religion, the loss from his doings has seemed greater than the gain. A fanatic, we are told, an enthusiast of narrow, if intense, vision who unloosed a tornado that he could not control, he turned what should have been peaceful evolution into revolution; he became the tool of unscrupulous secular princes and subjected the Church in half Europe to the State. Others have gone further and have conceived a dislike of Luther personally, even apart from his being a Protestant and a German. He was, they say, a boor, a sensualist, a man not of nice feelings who married a run-away nun and winked at bigamy in his patrons, an ill-bred person whose dash of sentimental religiosity added the most repulsive colouring to his acts.

These are serious charges. They are serious because there is a shadow of truth at least behind all of them. Luther was the most prominent figure in the revolution that split western Christendom and damaged many works of art. He did permit excessive control of Church affairs by secular princes when he thought he could trust them. He was a full-blooded man with a keen appreciation of the good things of this life. He kept to the end something of the roughness of the peasant stock of which he came.

But when all that can be said and more than can be proved has been set to Luther's discredit, he remains a great-hearted, great-souled man. He was more than that: he was a great man. His greatness was not the greatness of a theologian (though his contributions to theology were not so contemptible as is often assumed) nor was it the greatness of an ecclesiastical statesman. His was an odd kind of greatness, an unusual kind, but a real kind. His greatness lay in his personal religion. He was great in piety. He had that sort of intuitive knowledge of the situation of a devout soul which amounted to religious genius. And so it came about that the thing that mattered most about

Luther was not his theology or his churchmanship, but his personal experience of religion. That it is which gave him the position he holds and deserves in modern history.

Now one thing accounts for his enormous personal influence in his lifetime and the continuing importance of his religious experience for other men. Luther's experience was the typical, the characteristic experience of religion among the Christians of West Europe. The supreme religious experience came to him along the same lines as it has come at all times to those who have known it in the west. The fundamental religious interest of western Christianity is the quest for personal salvation: 'What must I do to be saved?' How can my life be put right, united, attain concord and effectiveness? How can I be sure that God, the power behind all life, is gracious? This last was Luther's problem; and if a soul as great as his, and yet as normal in its defects as well as its merits, could find a solution of the eternal problem of the ordinary Christian man, that solution was sure to have an influence both permanent and far-reaching.

To understand what Luther's experience was we must understand what sort of man Luther was. Subsequent events made Luther look like a radical revolutionary, a modern rebel against medieval ecclesiasticism; but if we look at Luther as he was, not as subsequent events made him appear, we shall find that in his inner nature he was a conservative, the fine product of medieval piety, precisely the kind of man the medieval Church existed to produce. Popular instinct has not erred in picturing Luther, first and last, as that most medieval of all figures—a monk (though in a technical sense he never was a monk).

Luther's experience did not begin with such dissatisfaction as provoked Wyclif. It began with his knowledge that something was wrong with himself, that he could not please God nor find peace. The theology in which he was trained led him to believe that by the sacrament of penance, if he was truly contrite, he could secure peace of mind and peace with God. This contrition he supposed he must find in his own heart. For a time he believed he had done so; later he saw that it was not true contrition, but only attrition, a sorrow that comes through fear of the consequences of sin, not through love of God.

Christ, he had learnt, had indeed died for our sins to reconcile us to God; but we received the benefits of the Passion through the sacrament of penance. If a man could feel only fear of punishment, not genuine heart-broken regret for sin, God's grace in the sacrament turned attrition into contrition. The worst was that the sacrament of penance itself brought to him neither, subjectively, the feeling that he could be sure was contrition nor, objectively, the unquestionable working of sacramental grace. Luther was at a loss what to do. He had entered the convent and renounced good prospects in the world because of doubt about winning his salvation there. Yet in the convent doubt still ruled him.

To his adviser Staupitz he owed direction in the way. Staupitz advised him to look for the commands of God not in books, but in 'the sweet wounds of the Saviour.' When Luther doubted of his personal predestination to eternal life or death, Staupitz again advised him, 'If you wish to dispute about predestination, begin from the wounds of Christ.' Not in what he could make of penance and penitence, but in what lay behind, making the sacrament of penance possible and giving it its meaning—there his main regard ought to be. Staupitz sent him to the Bible; that and St. Augustine's writings he studied.

So directed to look afresh at the Cross, Luther looked. It was not easy; it was not sudden; but there came a day for Luther like that day for St. Paul on the Damascus road or that for St Augustine in the Italian garden. As he read the Epistle to the Romans, the old, old miracle that time and again has happened in the history of the Church, happened yet once more. Scales fell from his eyes, and he saw the religious life as he had not seen it before. God in Christ had done all: 'He loved me, and gave himself for me.' There, in the wounds of Christ, where the Church in some way dim or clear has always pointed men, Luther saw what his own struggles had not shown him. He saw the Cross afresh, and like Bunyan's pilgrim he felt his burden roll away, and he saw it no more. Henceforth he had no doubt of the faith: of the place of the Cross in the work of salvation; of the little that man can do for himself; of the great thing that God has done for him. God's righteousness was no more the active righteousness by which he is just and punishes sin; it was the passive righteousness by which he mercifully makes us righteous by faith. We arrive at the classic phrase by which it became customary to describe Luther's experience: justification, being made righteous, by faith. It is important to see how we arrive at it: not by a factious quarrel with the Church or with dogma, but by the bitter-sweet experience of a great wounded soul struggling along the roads prescribed by the Church and suddenly finding peace where the Church had always said it was to be found. *Lord Jesus, King and Redeemer, save us by Thy Blood,* they have written over the door of Westminster Cathedral. It is written always everywhere over the deepest Christian experience. It was written on Luther's heart. *By Thy blood*: the deeper he felt it, the more impatient he became of every smaller explanation. Outside himself the work was done, and he who believes, he has it. *Wer glaubt, der hat.*

This experience made religion a new thing for Luther. He had thought of God as the punisher and Christ as the judge of sin. His own struggle against sin had seemed apart from both, and the very words *just* and *justice* were hateful to him. He had held the orthodox doctrine of the divinity and the humanity of Christ, but he had not found in it any meaning for his own life. Now he had learnt to connect the needs of his own life with the human figure of our Lord. By the contemplation of that figure he had found himself pardoned and comforted and mastered; and, because of that, he had recognized through the touch of Christ the touch of God. 'I have had,' he wrote later, 'so many experiences of Christ's divinity, that I must say: either there is no God, or he is God.' His complaint against the Roman Church was that it had held apart two things that ought to go together: forgiveness of sin and the apprehension of Christ's person. By supplementing the work of Christ with talk of human merit it had failed to show men the true significance of the doctrine which it taught about Christ, and which, in a sense, most men believed. 'Christ is not named Christ because he has two natures. What meaning has that for me? But he bears his lordly and comforting names because of the office and work he has taken on himself.' And if in Christ's office and

73

work Luther found peace for his soul, he found there too the only sure revelation of what God is. The Roman Church, he complained again later, has not made it clear 'that we ought to learn to recognize God in Christ.' It had described Christ in terms of God rather than God in terms of Christ, as if we could know God first from other sources and then could use our knowledge to describe Christ. To Luther it now appeared that the whole meaning of the Gospel was precisely the reverse of this method. 'The Scriptures begin very gently, and lead us on to Christ as to a man, then afterwards to a Lord over all creatures, and after that to a God. So do I enter delightfully and learn to know God.' Luther had learnt at last to understand, with what was for him the freshness of a discovery, the central and incomparable position that Christ holds in the Christian religion and in the believer's life. 'Wherefore,' said he, 'when thou wouldst know and treat of thy salvation, setting aside all speculations on the divine majesty, all thoughts of works, traditions, philosophy, and even the divine law, run straight to the manger and the mother's bosom, embrace that babe the little Son of the Virgin, and behold him being born, sucking, growing up, having conversation among men, teaching, dying, rising again, ascending up above all heavens and having power over all things.' This (though it is by no mean confined to circles called evangelical) is the great evangelical experience, and from it comes the great evangelical passion.

The essence of Luther's experience was, then, a personal not an ecclesiastical affair. In itself it was not controversial. So little did it provoke Luther to rush at once and assault the existing religious arrangements that scholars have had much doubt about the precise

74

moment at which he passed the landmarks. It was before any charge of unorthodoxy arose, probably about his thirtieth year. The decisive experience showed itself in his theological lecturing. He began to lay an emphasis on new places.

How, then, and why did religious revolution come from Luther? If the Church had had wiser, more disinterested rulers, Luther would never have made a breach, whoever else might have done so. But that the Church had neither wise nor disinterested rulers everyone agrees. Widespread corruption is admitted. The Pope was not a man of deep religious experience or understanding. He needed money to rebuild St Peter's Church in Rome, and to raise money a Dominican, Tetzel, came selling indulgences in Germany. Into the theology behind the sale of indulgences it is unnecessary to go. The practice had grown from small beginnings. If properly understood the purchase of an indulgence did not mean what ignorant men supposed; but there is no doubt that, whatever scholarly theologians taught about indulgences, many who bought them believed that by buying them they secured, not only freedom from suffering the penalties of their sins in purgatory, but God's forgiveness too without any change in their own hearts or intentions. Paying money, they supposed, affected God's attitude to them. Conscientious bishops and priests protested against the influence of hucksters like Tetzel who took no care to prevent misunderstanding. To Luther, fresh from his hardly-won knowledge of forgiveness, it appeared peculiarly monstrous that the ignorant should presume to buy and sell the pardon which came 'by thy blood.' He had no desire to rebel against the Church. He only criticized a practice which seemed to him to contradict what he had found to be God's word to his own soul and what, it seemed to him, the Church itself had taught about forgiveness. What he had learnt he had learnt from the Church.

In 1517 Luther nailed up on the door of the castle church at Wittenberg the famous ninety-five theses, statements that he wished to discuss and defend. The main contention in them was that whilst an indulgence, an arrangement of the Church, may on such terms as the Church appoints do away with any penalty appointed by the Church, it cannot take away guilt in God's sight. That, since God sees it there, he only can remove, and 'by thy blood' he has removed it. This was a far-reaching principle. It denied to the Church at a crucial point the power of acting in God's place. The Church could deal with men in this life alone. Luther was sure that he had at last understood the Church's teaching about the effect of Christ's death on our souls. He must prevent modern error from clouding the old, sound, true doctrine.

The rulers of the Church handled Luther badly. The papacy was not in 1517 spiritually minded enough to treat either Luther or Tetzel as it would have treated them a generation later or some generations before. It had to pay the price of all institutions which degenerate to low spiritual levels and do not keep their main object fully and exclusively in view. It did not know how to treat its own children. It could not even recognize them. Luther's piety and Luther's experience were essentially at one with medieval religion at its best; but the sixteenth century papacy had no understanding of medieval religion at its best and no use for it. Dr Eck, a typical ecclesiastical controversialist, came to drive off the field the insignificant professor whose protest against indulgences sanctioned by the Pope had aroused a most inconvenient turmoil throughout Germany. Eck was an abler disputant than Luther. He won a dialectical victory. He had no difficulty in driving Luther much farther than Luther had intended or wished to go. Innocent conservative as he had appeared at first, Luther was shown up as a heretic no better than Huss, Wyclif, the Waldenses, and the rest. Luther accepted what Eck had proved. If loyalty to the truth that he had found in the Church meant a break with Rome, a break with Rome must come. It was absurd to tell him he was parting from the Church in the very experience that first destroyed his old doubt about his belonging to it. The corrupt Italian court must not deny to the men of his own time that experience which he knew to be in the line of all great Christian experiences. There must be room in Christ's Church for forgiveness 'by thy blood.' Luther had a peasant's obstinacy and perhaps a peasant's narrow view; but it was not his fault that a peculiarly vivid knowledge of the central Christian experience set him at variance with the Society charged to guard that knowledge and induce that experience.

We need not follow Luther to the end of his career. After the disputation came the bull of excommunication. Luther burnt it, but when he did so neither Luther nor the Pope whom he defied knew that the general political situation in Europe was such that this defiance would result in a revolution without parallel. Luther deserves neither credit nor discredit for this. Papal abuses and the rise of the secular State made his career end, not as it normally would have ended, at the stake, but as leader of a reformed Church, suddenly called to improvize a new ecclesiastical system for people who valued his experience and wanted to share it. Now appeared the weaker side of Luther's work. He was not an ecclesiastical statesman. He had no fundamental quarrel with the Church as an institution. He had no new understanding of the meaning, the duties, and the privileges of churchmanship. His movement fell into the hands of secular governments. They exploited it, because it gave them an opportunity to carry out their policy of secularizing, destroying, and controlling various parts of the medieval Church. As an organization the Lutheran Church showed weakness and confusion. In some countries it became a tool of the secular State. In some it retained episcopacy; in some it did not. It used in different times and places more or less of the old rites, the old calendar, the old vestments and ornaments. It seemed to lack a guiding principle in such matters. Yet because it has had its feet firmly on the profoundest of Christian experiences, it has had power to survive its weaknesses and to outlive the governments that abused it. It remains strong where it has always been strong, in piety that springs from a contemplation of the deepest things we know.

How did all this affect England? What invigorating element has it introduced into English religion? How has it helped to counterbalance that weakening which we have considered? Expressed in one phrase, the work of Luther for England was to inspire whatever is meant by evangelical piety. We use the great word *evangelical* in its best and widest sense with reference to that vivid, direct experience which is very near the centre of Christ's Gospel. It is a scandal that controversialists, degrading words like 'evangelical' and 'catholic,' have given them the fustiness of party banners.

The inspiration of English evangelicalism inside and outside the Established Church goes back to Luther. It has shared both his weakness and his strength. It has rarely been clever at the machinery of politics. Outside as well as inside the Established Church it has sometimes lacked the instincts of the greatest churchmanship, the balanced judgement of what is and what is not essential for the well-being of the body as a whole, the sense of the value of the visible Divine Society, its need for unity, its demand for loyalty. The strength of evangelicalism has been in everything that makes for personal devoutness and communion with God, especially in devotion to the name and person of our Saviour. We find Luther himself and those whom he has inspired in England and elsewhere great in their use of the means of grace as personal means of grace, great in their use of prayer, great in their translation and study and circulation of the Bible, great in their composition and use of hymns. No one can doubt that among the finest hymns of Christendom are those written by Luther and those whom he has helped to his own faith. Beside the hymns of Lutheranism stand the hymns of John and Charles Wesley. Not less great have these men been in their use of the sacrament of the Supper of the Lord (to give it the name they loved). Their doctrine of this sacrament, their conception of its place in the public worship of the Church may be thought inadequate, but only purblind prejudice can discount the fervid piety with which they have received it or the passion with which they have adored through it the eternal Sacrifice.

Another side of evangelical influence has been seen in what is sometimes rather hideously called practical Christianity. Lovers of evangelical religion have not

79

planned the same assault upon the whole framework of society as Calvin did, but they have laboured much to remove or alleviate suffering. Evangelical religion has been a fountain-head from which, perhaps, more abundantly than from any other in the modern centuries, there has flowed an unbroken stream of orphanages, schools, hospitals, societies, and institutions for every conceivable purpose of charity, above all for foreign missions. In emphasizing this side of evangelicalism we must not minimize the vast work of other sections of Christendom, but the close connexion of the evangelical passion and the spread of missionary and charitable activities is an impressive feature of modern history.

Here, then, is one of the forces that has re-invigorated modern religion: intense personal piety stung into passion by a fresh sight of Christ's cross, supported by the devout use of the means of grace, and issuing in good works. We can follow this influence across all national and denominational frontiers. In England it shows itself in much of Cranmer's work in the Prayer Book, in the Methodist revival and the quickening of the old Dissenting Churches in the eighteenth century; in the evangelical tone of all nineteenth century Free Churches, whether Calvinist or Methodist in origin; in the evangelical party inside the Church of England; in enthusiasm for domestic charities and foreign missions. It is the same strain of personal religion that is illustrated in the Middle Ages in St Bernard of Clairvaux.

IV

JOHN CALVIN AND THE RESTATEMENT OF CHURCHMANSHIP

JOHN CALVIN is the supreme example of a man blessed because men say all manner of evil against him falsely for Christ's sake. No character more generally disliked at the present time can be found in the whole range of Church history. Everyone knows that he had some responsibility for burning Servetus, a man with an inadequate doctrine of the nature of Christ. Everyone associates him with a gloomy Puritanism and an inhuman doctrine of Predestination. Few have noticed that the first edition of the *Institutes* contains scarcely a trace of this particular doctrine, which is nevertheless often represented as the sum of Calvin's teaching. His whole attention in the first edition is given to the problems confronting a Christian society trying to live according to the law of God. Few indeed seriously attempt to understand what his doctrine meant. Fewer still consider that, in view of the doings of the other people in Europe with equal power and equal temptations in the matter of burning heretics, Calvin might well have been astonished at his own moderation. It would be difficult to name many temporal or ecclesiastical princes in the sixteenth century who were directly responsible for the death of only one man.

Calvin, it is true, had not the great tender heart, the fund of humour and human passion, that attract men to Luther, though he was not the severe misanthrope that his detractors and theological opponents make out.

Calvin's main claim on our attention is, however, not as an attractive personality but as a great churchman. As a churchman he merits not only our attention, but our gratitude. It will be well to pass over all smaller matters to make this clear. Important as was the whole of his theology, no other part was in the long run so important as that on which his doctrine of the Church rested. It is by his churchmanship that he has affected Europe most and longest and best.

If we seek to contrast Calvin's permanent work with Luther's we can do it in two phrases. It was Luther's work to illustrate afresh for Christendom what the hymn-book 'for the use of the people called Methodists' describes as 'the pleasantness and excellence of religion.' It was Calvin's work to illustrate afresh what the heading of the Authorized Version of Psalm xlviii calls 'the ornaments and privileges of the Church.'

For Luther all began, both weakness and strength, with the individual soul saved by faith. For Calvin the emphasis was different. What specially concerned him was not the process by which the individual soul found salvation. God's eternal decree had ordained that; whom he had foreknown, them he would call. What concerned Calvin was the company of the saved, the formation and the activity of the Divine Society on earth. The saved Church rather than the saved soul dominated his thinking and his living.

When in Chapter I we observed the wasting of the medieval Church by the modern State, the processes of secularization, destruction, and control, we noted, but did no more than note, that these changes affected thought as well as the material side of the legacy of the Middle Ages. We must now ask how thought was affected. The wasting process could not continue indefinitely and on so large a scale without moving some hearts to indignation and some minds to thought. The spoiling of the Bride of Christ, the subjection of her who had once been fair as the sun, clear as the moon, terrible as an army with banners, the prostitution of her by parvenu nobles, meanly lustful for her gold and her lands—these shameful deeds as they went on throughout all Europe roused in loyal churchmen of all schools of opinion resentment and resolve: resentment against the control of the Church by the State, and resolve to give back to the Church its ancient liberty. In Roman Catholic countries this re-assertion of Church rights was mainly the work of the Jesuits. In Protestantism it was the work of Calvin and Calvinists.

Calvin belonged to the generation that came after Luther's. He saw that unless the stream of enthusiastic personal religion set flowing by Luther's work found a more permanent and better planned channel than the rather haphazard institutions constructed by Luther two things must happen. First, Protestantism would become a mere creature of the secular State, the toy of politicians; worldly men would use the whole heritage of Christ for their own ends; and second, as a result of this, the feeling of all men with true love for Christ's kingdom on earth would drift back to the Church of Rome. That corrupt society despite all its faults would appeal to every man with a sense of churchmanship as at least still independent and self-respecting. The new, purer religious movements would be crushed out of existence. On the one side the secular State would degrade them; on the other the old corrupt Church would replace them. Nor was this all. It was likely that the Roman Church, in order to save itself in countries not yet lost, in France and Spain for example, would accept the domination of the State, and would place itself under secular patronage and control in as degraded a manner as Protestantism itself had done. Something like this did indeed happen in Roman Catholic countries in the seventeenth and eighteenth centuries. Until the revolutions of the nineteenth and twentieth centuries separated Church and State in many Roman Catholic countries, the Roman Church outdid even Anglicanism and Lutheranism in its subservience to the temporal powers. There was in the first centuries of modern history a very real danger that all sense of the independence of ecclesiastical societies would be lost in the west of Europe as it had already been lost in the east. There, with dire results, the Church had become little more than a department of State in charge of public worship. If this had happened in the west too, the State would have been left the only effective society in Europe, the great Leviathan of which Hobbes wrote. Western civilization would not have known that interplay of the claims of competing societies which has given the individual some freedom from them all. The struggle of the churches that were not under state control to obtain, despite the State, a foothold in national life produced religious liberty, and of the struggle for religious liberty political liberty is a by-product.

We can only imagine what would have been the course of the religious history of western Europe if some successful re-assertion of the rights of the Church had not been made against the State in the hey-day of its modern triumphs. The recent history of Christianity in eastern Europe shows but too vividly the woeful effects of the failure to make any such assertion. In the Byzantine Empire, as long as Constantinople withstood the Turkish hordes, the Church leaned too confidently on the friendly State, enjoyed too much patronage, and suffered too much control. In Russia of the Czars this story repeated itself. The eastern Church did not learn by asserting its inherent rights to stand in its own strength. All the Christians of the Greek communion enjoyed a spiritual union with one another, but their union had no centre of organic unity. When, therefore, in the near east and in Russia anti-Christian governments took the place of friendly governments the change in the secular world distressed and confused and broke up the Church beyond all telling. It had had no need to develop a strong independent organization of its own. It had not secured its own unity and its own resources by its own institutions. Today it is learning to stand alone, and in time it will provide itself with the necessary organization, but meanwhile much ground will be lost and centuries of work may be needed to recover it. The spirit and tradition and apparatus of ecclesiastical independence was much more highly developed in the west than in the east. This is one of the main lines of differentiation to be observed in the history of the Church.

To the medieval papacy in the first place and to John Calvin in the second place the Christian west owes much of its happier fate, its spirit of ecclesiastical independence and its possession of self-reliant corporations to express this independence. These characteristics mark Protestant and Roman Christianity alike and equally in the west; and, though neither is likely to admit it, each owes an enormous debt both to the medieval papacy and to John Calvin. The papacy prevented the Church from falling into dependence on secular princes in the Middle Ages, and in an age when the Popes were too badly discredited and too much engrossed in other matters to assert ecclesiastical independence their mantle fell on Calvin.

Calvin perceived that the greatest need of the sixteenth century was a positive ecclesiastical policy. It was idle to criticize the defects in the old Church in the manner of Wyclif. It was insufficient to arouse fresh piety among men in the manner of Luther. Only a Church with a claim and sphere as wide, an authority as august, a foundation as venerable and secure, a machinery as efficient, a policy as subtle, a temper as high, a mission as complete, could replace the corrupted Church of Rome and hold its own against the secular State rising everywhere on the ruins of medieval religion. Protestantism had produced prophets and preachers and theologians. It had not yet produced an ecclesiastical statesman, an architect on earth of that city whose builder and maker is God. In Calvin it produced him. From Geneva he planned a new Rome on lines as generous as the old. 'New presbyter,' said Milton as he surveyed Calvin's work, 'is but old priest writ large.' It was true. It hit the nail precisely on the head. In the sixteenth century the true successor of Popes like Gregory VII and Innocent III was not the Spanish chaplain who sat in St Peter's chair in Rome, but John Calvin who defied the kings and states of Europe with the old prophetic spirit and the old priestly authority: 'I have this day set thee to root out and to pull down . . . to build and to plant . . . the nation and kingdom that will not serve thee shall perish.'

What did Calvin's work mean for England? He inspired a number of Englishmen with his conception of the Church. They determined to establish it here and so to save the going concern from becoming the plaything of Tudor and Stuart politicians. These men are usually named Puritan, but when we think of their ideals for the Church it is better to call them Genevan, because their eyes turned to the Church organized by Calvin in Geneva as a model.

The essential feature of Calvin's conception of the Church we have seen. Religion was to be reformed; but reformation was not to be sought by lopping off those parts of the old Church that appeared corrupt and by making the best of the fragment that remained. It was necessary to view the whole situation afresh and to face the world not with a truncated Church, but with a Church capable of supplying every need that the old Church supplied, and wielding every weapon that it wielded. We can trace the parallel between Geneva and Rome throughout. To begin with, for Geneva not less than for Rome, *extra ecclesiam nulla salus*. The visible institution of the Divine Society must receive again in modern life the place that it had held in medieval. The Church is not one means among others by which God's grace can come to man: it is the only appointed way of salvation. Christian experience cannot be had apart from ecclesiastical institutions. Christian experience is ecclesiastical experience. The Church is not a help to religion: the Church is religion. It follows that its authority must be absolute. It is founded not on the doubtful, fabulous, corrupted line of succession from St Peter, but on the eternal decree which fore-ordained the elect to salvation. The Church is made of those who are the elect of God. God's choice gives them immediately, with no doubtful intermediaries, the utter security of the possession of the Holy Ghost.

The authority of the Church is in the whole company, the assembly of the faithful elect. Whatever power has been wrongly claimed by the Bishop of Rome may be rightly claimed by the whole Body of Christ. Christ's vicar, holding the keys of the kingdom of heaven, with power to bind and to loose, is the Church. The valid act is the act of the Church. People commonly say that, by contrast with Rome, Calvin substituted an authority that came from below, from the popular assembly, for an authority that came from above, from the Pope. That is the grossest error. For Geneva no less than for Rome all valid authority in the Church came from above; but it came by a different route. This authority no earthly prince or magistrate must claim or curtail. In every country where it appeared Calvinism defied the State, and either made advantageous terms with it, as in Scotland, or withdrew from its influence, as in England. Its unshaken confidence that it possessed divine authority enabled Calvinism alone to challenge the new monarchy in Europe and more than once to break its force.

With this clear-cut conception of the Church went of necessity a carefully graded hierarchy of ecclesiastical officials, both clerical and lay, quite unlike the almost haphazard arrangements of early Lutheranism. Nothing was left to chance. Every member of the faithful assembly had a voice in its decisions. All voices had not an equal influence, but each had a suitable influence. One Church court rose out of and supervised another. The system was capable of indefinite expansion. The full authority of the Divine Society, necessary for salvation, could be exercised as circumstances demanded by a tiny congregation alone in a hostile world, or by a national assembly, or by an ecumenical council.

The almighty Will which destined men for salvation willed also in any historical situation the adequate means.

We observed in Chapter I that the secular State destroyed or took over many of the functions of the medieval Church. In this way a whole side of ecclesiastical activities came to an end, notably those which disciplined the flock, which supervised their life from day to day, which prepared them for the reception of the sacraments, and which withheld the sacraments from the unworthy. This side of the matter did not escape Calvin. Learning from him the full duties and rights of the Church towards its individual members, Calvin's followers, more than any other Christians in West Europe, bewailed the loss of the godly discipline that the Church had once exercised, and clamoured everywhere for its restoration. In effect the secular State was claiming in many parts of Europe to decide on what terms citizens should be counted members of the new national Churches. This claim the Calvinists rejected. They declined to admit men who satisfied the demands of the secular state to full church privileges without further examination by the spiritual authority. They set up a system of discipline and enforced it through their church courts in defiance of the State when the State would not assist them. Tyrannical as this may have been in certain times and places, it was at least a recognition that Christendom could not do without a side of church life that was in no little danger of perishing completely. That only, in the famous phrase, is a true Church where the Word is faithfully preached, the Sacraments duly administered, and godly discipline enforced.

In some parts Calvin's work was less attractive and

perhaps less complete. His was not a genius to inspire the beautifully-expressed devotion of Lutheranism, nor had he much sense of what is called 'the art of public worship.' To people who are not Calvinists, Calvinistic worship has always seemed cold, bare, unlovely. It was not designed, it did not grow, with them in view. It was for the elect, and it has perhaps considered too little the impression that worship may make on the uninitiated. Calvinistic worship is not for the natural man. It is an acquired taste, but for those who acquire the taste it has an intensely satisfying quality. What the outsider calls its bareness—its austerity in ritual—depends ultimately on a fearful sense of the reality of all that the Church at worship does. To call on the Name of God, to claim the presence of the Son of God, if men truly know and mean what they are doing, is in itself an act so tremendous and so full of comfort that any sensuous or artistic heightening of the effect is not so much a painting of the lily as a varnishing of sunlight. The very phrase, 'the art of public worship,' with all the conceptions that lie behind it, is to men bred in Calvinistic worship something almost approaching blasphemy.

The plainness of Calvinistic worship has therefore in essence nothing in common with the informality of those groups of Christians who set little store on any external acts of worship. It has no kinship with the plainness of worship of the Society of Friends. Calvinistic rites are simple, not because they are of little or no importance, because they may be observed or may be neglected as individuals find best, or because they are half-way houses to no rites at all; they are simple because the grace of which they are the means is so irresistible that in their simplest form they are completely and eternally adequate. Elements, words, and faithful intention made the sacrament. To the Calvinist it was superfluous, and something worse than superfluous, to add to these.

It is perhaps in the power only of the few to breathe in that rare atmosphere. Incomparably august as the unencumbered worship is for them, for others it degenerates very quickly into coldness and slovenliness. Divine service among the Calvinists passed easily, when the spiritual temperature dropped, into a sort of public meeting. *Corruptio optimi pessima.*

V

THE FREE CHURCHES

WE are now in a position to ask what has made the religion and the irreligion of modern England, and to provide a partial answer. A large share in the making of both has come from the interaction of the forces we have examined: the destruction of parts of the medieval legacy, the adaptation of parts of it, the stimulus of two creative churchmen, Luther and Calvin.

One aspect of religion in modern England has been the Free Churches, Nonconformity, Dissent: those companies of Christians who left the religious organization that possessed most of the relics of the medieval legacy and claimed to find in other institutions a fuller church life, at times denying that the form of religion established by law was in any true sense a Church. These companies, apart from the particular names that have distinguished them, have borne in common negative names, *Dissenters* and *Nonconformists*, as if the main thing that differentiated them from the Established Church was some negative opinion, some denial, some refusal to accept what someone else affirmed. This suggestion is false. The foundations of this side of English religion are affirmations as positive as the foundations of any other. No movement as fruitful as English Nonconformity ever nourished itself mainly on negations. Nonconformists did indeed dislike many features in the Establishment that they left, but they left it to obtain an inheritance, not to avoid one.

What was the particular inheritance that they went out to seek? It was double: the evangelical passion that comes whenever Luther's experience is repeated and the ecclesiastical conviction that comes whenever Calvin's doctrine possesses a man. Almost all the Free Churches separated from the Establishment because inside it they could not find room fully to express one or other, or both, of these things. They may have been wrong, but that was their belief.

Nothing, however, is so misleading as to talk as if the Free Churches broke off in a sort of afterthought when the Anglican Church had already taken definite shape. Before Henry VIII had conceived of the break with Rome that gave the Church in England the opportunity of reconsidering its position, Luther had had his evangelical experience, and twelve years before the first English Prayer Book appeared Calvin had written his *Institutes*. The influence of both Luther and Calvin had been long in the world and had dominated many Englishmen before the Anglican Church under Queen Elizabeth took its present form. If no sects were established immediately to express the new ideas, it was because neither the Lutheran nor the Genevan party had abandoned hope of securing control of the existing Church establishment and of expressing their ideas through it. That hope held some of them till 1662. Others, seeing the struggle hopeless, had begun earlier to establish sects or to go to America. 1662 is a landmark in the history of Nonconformity because in that year the action of Charles II's government permanently convinced a great many people that the Established Church would not provide scope for the kind of church life that they intended to live. In the course of the next century another great section

93

of the Established Church became convinced that the Establishment did not provide the full religious life they needed; but in the eighteenth century it was the devotional life inspired by the evangelical experience that could not be satisfied.

We have then two new forces in modern English religion which fail to find satisfactory expression in the Established Church and cause two main groups of secession: the sixteenth and the seventeenth century secession, culminating in 1662, for the sake of Genevan churchmanship, and the eighteenth century secession, for the sake of the evangelical experience. The two movements of course were not watertight, but the distinction, though not absolute, is accurate. One quality the two movements had in common. They both conceived a sharp cleavage between society in general and the Church. In their opinion the Church was a 'gathered Church,' separate from the world. The Established Church has never entirely abandoned the medieval view that the Church is the religious aspect of the whole of a Christian society, though in recent years it has organized itself more and more as a 'gathered Church,' separate and easily distinguishable from the general society of the parish or the nation.

It is time to come to names, to denominations. The Free Churches of today which most directly represent the endeavour to express the full churchmanship of John Calvin are the ancient 'Three Dissenting Bodies,' Presbyterians, Congregationalists (or Independents), Baptists. All were hewn from the Genevan rock or digged from the Genevan pit. They are of the same stock, marked by minor differences. They all belong to the earlier secessions of the sixteenth and seventeenth centuries. Though some of them never accepted the

94

Tudor settlement of religion as a possible shape for the Church, others did not abandon it till 1662. The Baptists differ from the Presbyterians and Congregationalists in administering baptism to adults only, deeming it a sign of admission to the full rights of church membership. Presbyterians and Congregationalists agree with one another and with almost all other Christians in baptizing infants, deeming it a sign of their redemption by Christ and of their position as potential, if not active, members of his Church. This potential membership becomes active when, at what may be said in some way to correspond with confirmation in the episcopal communions, they are admitted to full church fellowship. The Presbyterians lay more emphasis on the linking of the separate congregations than the Congregationalists (and Baptists), but Presbyterianism and Congregationalism are only centralized and decentralized expressions of the same Calvinistic doctrine of the Church. In their fundamental conceptions of the composition, the powers, the sacraments, and the ministry of the Church they are at one. Both have made use of the Westminster Confession of Faith. They stand for the same high notions of churchmanship and a regular use of the sacraments with what they believe to be apostolic austerity.

The second great group of Free Churches is the Methodist. Methodism sprang for the most part from the work of John Wesley. Formerly the Methodists were divided into many denominations, Wesleyan, Primitive, Free, and so on, but now they are about to reunite. Not having the same ecclesiastical dissatisfaction with the Establishment as the earlier Dissenters had had, the Methodists at first called themselves only a Society and tried to retain their membership in the Established Church. Controversialists often say that John Wesley never intended to break away from it and that his followers have defied his wishes. John Wesley, it is likely, neither wished nor planned a severance; but he accepted the fact of a severance. He had both a High Church and a High Calvinist ancestry, an ancestry incompatible with loose notions of Church order. Down both lines he had learnt what the sacred ministry and the rite of ordination meant. It is inconceivable that he did not realize that he had parted company from the Episcopalians and accepted the Presbyterian doctrine of the ministry when he, a presbyter, ordained men. John Wesley always knew what he was doing.

Though the Methodist movement made necessary an ecclesiastical break, its origin was not in a doctrine of the Church, but in an experience of personal religion. Wesley, like Luther, had an experience of direct access to God and to peace of soul. He had as little quarrel as Luther with his Church. His Church handled him with as little understanding, and reaped the same reward.

But unlike Lutheranism and unlike the kindred and contemporary Evangelical movement inside the Established Church, the Methodist Society did not suffer from any lack of statesmanship. In John Wesley the Methodists had a leader who, by a stroke of divine genius that puts him in the same rank as Hildebrand, St Dominic, and St Ignatius Loyola, combined the evangelical passion and experience of Luther with Calvin's ecclesiastical system. The result of his work was (if it be considered merely as an organization) perhaps the most perfect piece of institutional machinery in the modern world. The Wesleyan Methodist Church, though making great use of laymen for preaching and administration, is a highly centralized and slightly clerical type of Presbyterianism. Its clericalism and centralization were too much for some, who felt the evangelical passion without the need for so dominant an organization; and so appeared the divisions which are now being healed. The unique strength of Methodism comes from its marvellous use of both the new creative forces in modern religion.

Two other things it is necessary to say about the Free Churches. First, the evangelical movement in the eighteenth century which created Methodism and revived Anglicanism did not miss the old Dissenters. They caught a more vivid passion than they had known, and like the Methodists came to enjoy the heritage of Luther as well as Calvin. In this is the underlying cause of the movement to reunite all the Free Churches. They no longer represent separate springs of religious life. They all draw from all.

Second, there is a school of religious thought apart from the main line of the Free Churches which is seen in its most characteristic form in the Society of Friends. It differs fundamentally from those we have already considered in assigning to the institution of the visible Church, its sacraments and its ministry, a less important place in the Christian life. It regards the Church as a help to the religious life, but not as its essence. This school of thought has influenced people in the Free Churches as well as in the Established Church, but it has no more affinity with historic Dissent than it has with historic Anglicanism. In so far as it forms societies and shapes opinion rather than embodies itself in a Church it falls outside the province of this book.

VI

THE ANGLICAN CHURCH

IT may appear odd in a discussion of English religion to leave till the last the Church which during the whole of the period covered has commanded the allegiance of most religious Englishmen. It was necessary in order to get the historical background to deal first with the positive influences of Luther and Calvin. The Established Church did not produce many constructive thinkers until the work of Luther and Calvin had already taken effect in England, and it would have been awkward to have to retrace our steps to them.

Even when a consideration of Luther and Calvin has prepared the ground it is not easy to discuss Anglicanism. Anglicanism is so thoroughly English as to be extremely tiresome to describe. With the possible exception of Cranmer, whose work has been unduly depreciated, we cannot find in sixteenth-century Anglicanism great creative names to set beside those of Luther and Calvin in continental Protestantism or that of St Ignatius Loyola in continental Romanism. Beside these the Englishmen look small, not to be sure in personal merit but in the results of their individual efforts.

People take very different views of the relation of the modern Established Church to the medieval Church in England, but whatever his view no one denies that there was a crisis in English religion early in the sixteenth century. Let us remind ourselves of the equipment with which the Established Church appeared after that crisis.

First, on the institutional side it took over so much of the going concern of medieval religion as was not destroyed or secularized: the parish churches, endowments, the clergy, the prestige. The price paid was state control; for upon destruction, secularization, *or* control, the Tudor State had determined. How effective the control was may be judged from such matters as (1) the undisputed control of the secular government over all important Church patronage and the cessation of all but the form of the canonical election of bishops, though respect for canonical election had been one of the main objects of churchmen for many centuries; (2) the lightning changes of policy and ritual under Henry VIII and his children: from 1530 to 1560 the Established Church hardly knew for five years together precisely what doctrine it would be called on to confess or what ritual to observe; (3) the silence and almost the abandoning for many generations of the official organ for the expression of church opinion, Convocation—a condition without many parallels in the history of Christendom.

Second, inside the institutional equipment was the spiritual equipment. This was double: traditional religion and contemporary religion, neither to the exclusion of the other. The Established Church presented Christian doctrine, and life as it was received by tradition from the early and the medieval Church and by the new direct experience characteristic of the age. A familiar poem[1] describes the situation under the form of a contrast of the Roman and the Genevan Church as women: she of the seven hills arrayed in

1 George Herbert, *The Temple*, The British Church.

tawdry flashy clothes and ornaments, she of the Genevan valley so prudish as to wear nothing whatever. The English Church arrayed herself in a decent and comely fashion midway between the two styles.

If we examine more closely what came to the Anglican Establishment down each line we find that from the medieval side, apart from the going concern, came the general form of ritual and the threefold ministry of bishops, priests, and deacons. Certainly the substance of what Borrow called 'England's sublime liturgy' is due to the inspiration of medieval service books; but whether the threefold ministry of the Anglican Establishment is a valid continuation of the medieval ministry is a question answered differently by Anglicans and Roman Catholics. Before we can arrive at an historical view of the relation of the Anglican Establishment and the Free Churches with the medieval Church in England we must observe the relation of the modern Roman Church with the medieval Church. This relation is by no means so simple or so plain as most controversialists on each side used to assume and as some still wish to assume.

Attempts have been made from time to time to show that the Church in England in the Middle Ages stood in some very peculiar relation to the See of Rome; but it seems clear that England was a part of the communion of western Christendom with essentially the same relations with Rome as any other part. In England as in other countries these relations changed and developed as centuries passed. England was more remote and more undeveloped than some parts of western Christendom. This condition affected ecclesiastical communications; the connexion with Rome may have been loose and uncertain at times, but that was all. The extreme claims of the English ecclesiastical nationalists seem exaggerated.

But it does not necessarily follow from this that the Roman controversialist is right in the controversy that breaks out periodically about the claim of the modern Roman Church in England to be the only true representative of medieval English religion. The Roman controversialist is right in arguing that all attempts to minimize the changes of the sixteenth century are futile and that a very decisive revolution in English relations with the See of Rome then occurred. Modern Christians in western Europe not in communion with the Bishop of Rome do differ from their medieval predecessors in a matter that their medieval predecessors regarded as extremely important. But if the Church in England, including those who became Dissenters, suffered notable changes in the sixteenth century, so did the Roman Church. *Tu quoque* is not a retort: here it is an argument. It is fairly easy for the Roman controversialists to show that the Venerable Bede or St Anselm, for example, did not hold all the theological positions of the modern Anglican who claims to succeed them: they did not, for example, confess all that is confessed in the Thirty-Nine Articles; but it is equally easy to show that many orthodox medieval churchmen did not hold all the theological positions of the modern Roman Catholic who claims to succeed them: they did not, for example, confess that the Blessed Virgin Mary was immaculately conceived; they did not receive as canonical all the books of the Apocrypha; they did not receive and venerate with an equal feeling of devotion and reverence books so dissimilar as *Tobit* or *II Maccabees* and the Four Gospels. If it is likely that orthodox medieval churchmen would have denied some tenets of modern Anglicanism or modern Dissent, it is certain that they combated some doctrines of the modern Roman Church.

We need not pursue the controversy nor even enter it; but it is relevant to set out these aspects of it in order to avoid a common error. We are not to think of the period of the Reformation as a time when one great section of Christendom stood still in its ancient ways and held the faith of the past (whether those ways and that faith are considered corrupt or authoritative matters not) whilst rash or inspired persons like Luther and Calvin made a completely new start; and cautious men like Cranmer made a cunning compromise between what moved and what stood still. Controversialists on each side have often so drawn the picture, agreeing about the mobility and immobility of the parties, differing only in apportioning praise and blame.

Any such picture is false. At no time was any part of Christendom standing still. In the sixteenth century every part was moving very fast, not least the Roman Church. At the Council of Trent the Roman Church definitely closed to itself certain lines of development in thought and action which had hitherto stood open and had been used profitably in the Middle Ages. Every student of the history of doctrine must feel as he passes from the medieval to the modern Roman Church a quite definite narrowing of outlook, a cramping of action, a throwing overboard of some things formerly much prized. The Roman Church after the sixteenth century was less corrupt, freer from scandals, more devoted to its spiritual work, more efficient in its administration; but it was less free intellectually, less bold in its use of all the treasures of the Christian tradition, more fearful of exploring some of the un-searchable riches of Christ than it had been before the Council of Trent. It definitely refused to carry with it into modern times some parts of its ancient and medieval heritage. This happened partly from reaction against Protestantism. The doctrines of grace and predestination provide an example. In the Middle Ages it had been possible for orthodox churchmen to hold either of two views and to approach almost as near to St Augustine's position as the Protestants did. But in modern times at the Council of Trent the interpretation of the doctrine of grace favoured by Protestants was banned. To read St Augustine too much was likely to rouse suspicion; and if Archbishop Bradwardine had published his *De Causa Dei* in the seventeenth century he could hardly have avoided condemnation for heresy.

To say that the Roman Church has moved is not to blame it. Churches, if they are to live, must move. But it is idle to deny movement or to attribute it all to one side of modern Christendom. We have noticed these aspects of sixteenth-century history not because of modern controversies between the Roman and the Protestant Churches, but in order to understand why the Anglican Establishment took a middle position between Rome on the one side and the Lutheran and Genevan tradition on the other, and what justification it could allege for taking it.

Now its main reason and its main justification were not in the virtue of compromise. In religion com-promise is not a virtue. When Anglicanism has thought of itself as a gentlemanly compromise between the vulgarity of continental popery and 'the squalid sluttery of Dissenting conventicles' it has been at its lowest spiritual ebb. The justification of the Anglican refusal to move with the modern Roman Church down the ever-narrowing path lighted by the Council of Trent, St Ignatius Loyola, St Alphonsus Ligouri, and the Vatican Council is that the Anglican Church wished to keep open certain possibilities of development offered by the fullness and richness of Christian tradition in antiquity and the Middle Ages, possibilities which Rome now refused.

Even Anglicanism, by the *via media*, could not keep open all the doors of development. It had paid a certain price to obtain one most valuable part of the medieval religious legacy. In order to obtain the going concern and all that that meant in continuity of ritual and order and associations, it had renounced communion with the See of Rome and had accepted state control. That is to say, in order to obtain one part of the medieval religious legacy it had renounced another part, ecclesiastical independence and the liberty of churchmanship. That particular part of the medieval legacy fell, as we have seen, in England to the Calvinists, who paid a heavy price in the loss of continuity in church order for what they retained in continuity of church freedom. In the sixteenth century no one of the sections into which the medieval Church had broken could secure the whole of the medieval legacy. It is a common delusion that those who stayed in communion with Rome did secure it all at the price of a little temporary corruption. The history of the Council of Trent and the Vatican Council makes that opinion untenable.

Anglicanism, then, in taking a path that led to a break with the Roman See, did more than open a way for some of the new evangelical passion which was one of the best things that modern religion had to give: it left open also a way for a re-exploration of Christian antiquity, of the period of the undivided Church before East and West were severed, and even of the Middle Ages themselves, such a re-exploration as the modern Roman Church will not permit herself. Nor had Anglicanism assimilation from the present and the past alone in view. In parting from Rome Anglicanism did what Calvin also was anxious to do: it kept its doors open to the new learning of the Renaissance and to any newer that might follow it.

Having examined the relation of the Anglican Church to medieval Christendom and modern Romanism, let us see what it took from continental Protestantism. A part of its debt to Luther we noticed in the eighteenth-century development of the evangelical party; but in the sixteenth, partly through Cranmer's correspondence with Lutheran divines and sympathy with Lutheran thought, Anglicanism acquired some of its prominent features. Medieval service books inspired the substance of the Prayer Book, but that Anglicanism has its liturgy in the vernacular is in part due to the result of continental contemporary Protestantism. We probably owe the English Bible far more to Luther's work than to Wyclif's. It may be that with or without Luther an English liturgy and Bible would have come but, however they might have come, their historical appearance corresponded in time with Lutheran influence in England. To Luther too, directly and indirectly, it appears, Cranmer owed no little in the development of one side of his mysterious doctrine of the Eucharist: this asserted a real presence of Christ in the elements but did not commit itself to that philosophical explanation of the mystery, transubstantiation, which late medieval thought had worked out and which presents peculiar difficulty unless late medieval philosophy is held in its entirety.

To Calvin Anglicanism owed less than to Luther. Calvin's theology did indeed dominate much Anglican theology as most other English theology until the eighteenth century, but it was not worked permanently into the life of the Church as Luther's contribution was. And the main gift of Calvinism to Christendom —its vivid churchmanship, its winning back of ecclesiastical independence—the Anglican Church could not receive because it was unwilling to pay the price. It is possible to pay too high a price even for a good thing, and the Anglican Church judged the price too high.

Except Cranmer, and we may say that Anglicanism was not the creation of prophets; some (but they are too severe) would not even except him. Anglicanism took its shape from unprophetic, rather profane hands. We hear much of the King's Majesty and the Queen's Majesty; *Thus saith the Lord* sounds rather faintly in the Tudor settlements. But, however it took shape, the shape that Anglicanism took was so admirable that though men had accepted it on the authority of the Crown they came to love it for itself. Apologists for Anglicanism, inspired by the excellence of what they had to defend, turned prophets after the event. Judicious Hooker and Andrewes and Herbert, and the whole school of the Caroline divines, were men whom the chaste beauty of the Book of Common Prayer, the decency, the purity, the restrained but glowing devotion of the Church of England won to a loyalty that no royal edict could have commanded. Odd methods may have given the Anglican Church power, may even have called it into being; but once placed, it stood quite solidly on its own merits. And its merits in the judicious, loving eyes of these its sons, the Caroline divines, were precisely those merits which our examination of its relation with the Roman Church has prepared us to expect. The Caroline divines loved 'this Church of England' not mainly as a national institution, but because they saw in it more fully than in any other Church in Christendom the rich heritage of all Christian experience, ancient and medieval and modern. Here was the tradition of the ancient Church before the Bishop of Rome asserted his unbrotherly superiority over other metropolitans. Here was all save the corruption of the medieval Church. Here was Renaissance learning. Here was the direct, simple approach to the Gospel that the Reformers had reopened. They loved the great Church Catholic but (in the words of the Cambridge bidding prayer) 'especially that pure and reformed part of it established in this kingdom.' Its sad subjection to the secular State they somehow contrived to overlook.

There came a day when they could overlook it no longer. The Anglicanism of Queen Elizabeth's settlement had survived the Genevan attack of the seventeenth century. It had retained its grip on the going concern. The eighteenth century brought no ecclesiastical crises, but a new enriching of devotion by evangelical piety. But with the growth of Toleration and the steady secularizing of political life, with the divorce of English citizenship from English churchmanship (so that a man might possess the one and neglect the other), Anglicans had to reconsider the relation of their Church to the State. The going concern, with the momentum of the

Middle Ages, had carried this very charming but perhaps slightly invertebrate Anglicanism to the beginning of the nineteenth century, but there was every sign that it would go little further. The momentum, the prestige, the money of the Middle Ages would not be adequate much longer, even if the Anglican Church could keep them all. That it could keep them was by no means certain. Whig politicians played with the idea of disestablishment. The social prestige and political privileges that had enticed all luke-warm persons into the Anglican communion for non-religious reasons were coming to an end. Toleration was passing into the secular State. The Anglican Church might sink, as far as its legal and social status was concerned, into the position of one sect among the rest. But despite its greater size it would have this disadvantage: whereas they, with all their shabbiness and poverty, had always stood in their own strength, owing nothing to the State, usually indeed opposed by it, Anglicanism had never yet been driven to stand by itself relying exclusively on its religious resources.

What would happen if Anglicanism had so to stand? Could it? How adequate would be its appeal to the Christian conscience of England if the national, social appeal failed? Questions and doubts of this kind led the men who were to be the leaders of the Oxford Movement to probe to their foundations and see what strength they had; and in looking at the foundations that existed, they opened (if a mixed metaphor be permitted) new springs for the life of the Church. Following the example of the Caroline divines, the men of the Oxford Movement looked for inspiration to the early Church and the undivided Church, of which they believed the Anglican Church to be the best representative in Christendom. Nor did they look in vain. They found more than the inspiration they had expected. So well had Cranmer done his work.

Apart from its privileged position in the State, the Anglican Church, it appeared, had a reason to exist. Its justification and its strength lay mainly in two qualities: first, its alleged continuity (in which it at least believed) with the historic Church of the pre-Reformation period; and second, its alleged conformity (in which, again, it at least believed) with the ancient, uncorrupted church of the centuries before Constantine. Of these qualities the first, continuity, was thought to distinguish it from the Protestant Dissenting Churches, and the second, conformity with the pure model of primitive Christianity, was thought to disinguish it from Roman Catholicism, covered as it was by the accretions of centuries.

At first these two qualities stood equally prominent before the men of the Oxford Movement. Their early studies were mainly in the Fathers of the first four centuries. It was from the inspiration of that first impact of grace on humanity that they drew strength. 'Bliss,' they felt, 'was it in that dawn to be alive'; and they lived again in the light that still streamed from the open tomb of Christ before the blueness of distance had obscured it. We can feel it in their own hymns, in their translations of the early Greek and Latin hymns, and in their strict, scholarly, slightly prim delight in an austere but correct ritual. They were hardly ritualists in the later, more full-blown meaning of the word. They were theologians first, ritualists afterwards. They cared more that men should hold, for instance, the full faith in what the Eucharist is, or in what Holy

Orders convey, than that a particular vestment should be worn or a particular practice observed. Most of them were severely free from that more than feminine sentimentalism, often mixed with extreme ignorance, which marked some of their successors.

As time passed a change came. Stress was laid less on conformity with the ancient catholic and more on continuity with the medieval Latin Church. The defence against Rome became less vigorous, perhaps less confident. The differentiation from the Protestant Dissenters became more rigid. There grew to be some danger that the third characteristic feature of historic Anglicanism might be forgotten or overlooked: the care with which it had kept open for itself those doors to new and old knowledge that the Roman Church after the Council of Trent had barred against itself. Continuity with the Middle Ages ceased to be enough. Conformity with them was desired, and there were borrowings (as for instance of the service of Benediction) even from the non-medieval Romanism that followed the Council of Trent. Some of the issues of their work would have surprised the early Tractarians. We cannot approach contemporary events nearer without passing from history to controversy.

If on one side these latest developments of the Oxford Movement seemed likely to obscure one of the historic features and sources of strength of Anglicanism, and to bind on it restrictions that Cranmer had declined, on another side the Oxford Movement helped to give to the Anglican Church what Cranmer had not given it and what it had not hitherto had. Anglicanism began to achieve some faint beginnings of ecclesiastical independence, not in the full Roman or Calvinistic sense, but enough to mark at least an improvement on conditions before the nineteenth century. Church assemblies began to meet more effectively. The Church began, too, to rely for the maintenance and extension of its work not only on what it had inherited as a national institution, but to some extent on what the faithful voluntarily offered. Their gifts increased its material strength, its buildings and its endowments. Anglicanism is still deeply branded with Erastianism, but the Oxford Movement made it aware of the stigma.

There had already been a notable anticipation of the work that the Oxford Movement was to do for Anglicanism. The Non-Jurors showed where its weaknesses lay and on what lines they might be met. Their movement died from lack of recruits, but it was not without influence in inspiring others to attempt the same task in a different way.

Viewed from a certain angle the Revolution of 1688 seemed already to have achieved the worst results that the leaders of the Oxford Movement, more than a hundred years later, feared from disestablishment, disendowment, and the complete secularization of the State. James II might have been unworthy of his position, but he was the divinely-appointed governor of the English Church and the English State. The men who became Non-Jurors felt that when he was replaced by a Calvinistic Dutchman the old compact between Church and State had been destroyed. Anglicanism had not indeed lost its endowments and legal privileges in 1688. Worse had happened. By its acquiescence in what Parliament, the secular authority, had done the Established Church seemed to have sunk to a position intolerable for any true churchmanship. A small band of enthusiasts, therefore, declined to swear allegiance to the new settlement, and in the eye of the law they became Dissenters, incapable, like Presbyterians, of holding office in the Established Church. For more than a generation they maintained their ecclesiastical organization. They developed a type of doctrine and liturgy which may be considered a revival of the high churchmanship of the Caroline Divines or an anticipation of that of the Oxford Movement. As the partisan memories of 1688 died away their numbers dwindled, and as a sect they disappeared.

Though political attachment to the House of Stuart was the most immediately obvious feature of the Non-Jurors, they stand in the history of religious thought for something more worthy of respect and more permanently important. They asserted two things: first, that no secular authority has power to change the life or the doctrine—even the political doctrine—of the Church; and, second, that in order to maintain the true character of Anglicanism it had become necessary to emphasize that side of it which differentiated it from continental and Dissenting Protestantism. The legal persecution of the Dissenters since Charles II's Restoration had driven into the Established Church all but the most convinced opponents of the Elizabethan Settlement. The men who had conformed under pressure had not altered but only suppressed their opinions. To this school of thought the Revolution of 1688 was likely to allow more influence both inside and outside the Church. There was danger that the nice balance between Rome and Geneva would be lost. The Non-Jurors' movement was a reaction against this danger.

The accidents of the historical situation made the

Non-Jurors peculiarly unfortunate in both matters. Fate never showed itself more ironical than when it gave them as a symbol of the inviolable rights of their Church a Roman Catholic prince who despised it; and the immediate result of their stand for a higher doctrine and practice of churchmanship was to lower both. Their secession, more perhaps than anything else, gave control to precisely those schools of thought in Anglicanism which they conceived were already too powerful. One large body of clergy of orthodox theology and the highest notions of church authority and independence had been ousted from the Establishment in 1662. In 1689 another body of orthodox high churchmen was ousted. In many ways these differed from one another, but in their essential doctrine of the Church they differed still more from the dominant party that they left in possession. After such losses there was little marvel that the Established Church sank into Erastianism and Deism, into low notions both of the Church and of its Gospel. To the Non-Jurors, the Evangelicals, and the Oxford Movement alike, though not equally, belongs the glory of showing it the way from both.

VII

THE HISTORICAL APPROACH TO ECCLESIASTICAL PROBLEMS

WHAT can a study of history do for the elucidation and settlement of ecclesiastical problems? It can provide no short cut which theologians and statesmen have missed. It is doubtful if through history we can arrive at positive truth or at a definite solution of any practical problem. He knew much about history who said that, whenever he heard the words *All history teaches*, he was prepared to be told some tremendous lie. History provides no answers to conundrums, but it can put men into the right frame of mind for an approach to the problems of religion.

Religion on one side concerns itself with men. The historian can remind students of religion of certain features in human nature that they easily forget. Ill-founded optimism, the mother of despair, besets many people who study the development of religious opinion. They treat the subject simply as a clash of ideas and ideals. They assure themselves that if an opinion is true or good, it will survive and triumph. In the long run it may do so, but the historian notes that the run is sometimes very long indeed. There is acute danger of underestimating the influence of force and civil government and unspiritual apparatus on religion. The machinery of civil society cannot fall into irreligious hands without the gravest consequences for religion. In the study of the decline of Christianity in the Near and Middle East, for example, too much attention has gone to demerits in the faith and practice of the Eastern Church, too little to the military situation, the proximity of deserts and steppes, the movement of peoples—forces over which moralists and bishops have no control. The historian brings the study of religion back to earth, and whispers that the Church may have worse enemies than those denounced by conservative dignitaries or fanatical reformers. The seed is the Word of God, but the field is the world. To know the world, to measure and to use its forces, is not to dishonour the seed, but to care for it. High-minded ignorance about soils and a fine contempt for the fowls of the air may pass for evidence of a spiritual mind, but result in poor husbandry. The historian stoops to inquire if a well-placed scarecrow has not done service on occasion, and has a good word for the boy who, though only to amuse himself, brings down as many birds as he can with his gun. Without a constant breeze and an occasional blast from the fields of profane history the student of religion becomes too nice and too precious. He plays, like a dilettante, with fire and blood.

The historian not only calls attention to unpleasing facts. It is his work too to look without spectacles, or at least with a change of spectacles, at certain things already much examined by students of religion. The conception of *continuity* in the Church provides an example. No word occurs more often in ecclesiastical discussions. Ecclesiastical bodies are thought to be distinguished from one another by the possession of this quality or the lack of it. Controversy blazes from attempts to determine into which category any particular ecclesiastical body falls. But what is continuity? An historical approach to the question reveals that

there is among ecclesiastical bodies today continuity
of more than one kind, that no one of the sections into
which the Western Church has fallen since the fifteenth
century can successfully claim the whole inheritance
of the medieval Church, that none of them has complete
continuity, and that none is completely destitute of it.
Different bodies appear to possess more or less continuity according to the standard that is used.

Judged by the standard of church order one of the
modern bodies has a plain advantage. The modern
Roman Church preserves communion with the traditional see of St Peter at Rome and the threefold
ministry of bishops, priests, and deacons. The Church of
England possesses the second only of these forms of continuity. The other Churches in England possess neither.

The kind of continuity most immediately impressive
to the historian is, however, not church order. He sees
continuity first in those bodies that have inherited
from the medieval Church control of the going concern.
Revolutions in theology or church order, however
dramatic, do not prevent the historian from perceiving
that the Established Church in any country—Roman,
Anglican, Lutheran, or Calvinist—has fulfilled many
of the same functions in society as the medieval Church
and has stood in private and public life for many of
the same influences. This was especially true in the
earlier centuries of modern history before the importance
of the going concern had much diminished. From the
point of view of church order the harassed Jesuit
mission-priest in seventeenth-century England may
have been in the same line of continuity as the comfortable prince-bishops of the Roman Catholic Rhineland,
but from other points of view, not less important to
the historian, the heretic bishops of the Anglican

Establishment in Durham and Ely provided examples of a more effective kind of continuity. The theologian may ignore points of similarity in breeding, education, outlook on life, and influence on society, but the historian cannot. In these things, no less than in church order, there is true continuity.

Someone will say that the historian is too secular. But, when the historian turns to the more specifically religious character of ecclesiastical bodies, questions of church order by no means cover all the ground on which he sees continuity. Beside the order which provides the framework of the body there is the conscious spirit animating the body, the sense of churchmanship. To be intensely aware of personal membership of the Divine Society, to value and to use the privileges which separate its members from the world, to recognize and to be exercised by its discipline, to assert its rights against all other authorities, and to resist the efforts of external powers to control its affairs—a conscious churchmanship of this kind is as important a feature in the Christian society as is its order; and for the fullest continuity of this kind the historian has to look to a group of bodies quite different from those which show him continuity in order. The Churches which were inspired by John Calvin's restatement of churchmanship—the Presbyterian, the Congregational, and the Baptist—provide the plainest continuity of Church consciousness in modern England. To speak (as persons in other respects competent still speak) of the Anglican settlement as a mean between the too rigid, imperial discipline of Rome and the 'purely individualistic' Puritan conception of Christianity is to placard ignorance of the whole influence of Geneva in ecclesiastical history.

More fundamental perhaps than even order and church consciousness, and nearer to the very essence of Christ's religion, are doctrine and devotion. And here again the historian follows lines of continuity. He makes a rough, but not the less valid, distinction between those who preserved orthodox doctrine (however that may be described) when they broke with the regular ecclesiastical order of their time and country, and those who did not. To trace continuity in orthodox doctrine leads the historian to ecclesiastical bodies that utterly abandoned that particular continuity which the going concern and church order can give. Certain Socinians who have formally retained Episcopacy and certain Episcopalians who have substantially adopted Socinianism have doubtless preserved a kind of continuity of order; but in abandoning beliefs about the Person of the Saviour, held by all others who profess themselves Christians, they have clearly lost continuity of another, and probably more valuable, kind.

Continuity in methods of devotion is also a reality. It exists not only in liturgical forms of public worship, but even more in the intimate contemplation of those things from which passion and adoration spring. If the historian of eighteenth-century England looks for continuity in contemplation of the incidents and instruments of the Passion as means of devotion, he does not find it best where the threefold ministry regarded with suspicion whatever savoured of enthusiasm. He finds it among those who abandoned continuity of order to preserve continuity of devotion. It was among the Methodists mainly, after a lapse of centuries, that the labourers of Lincolnshire began to sing again, as they had sung in the Middle Ages, of the Five Wounds of

Christ, and to find in contemplation of his cross a passionate piety that expressed itself in words ringing more consonantly with the richest medieval devotions than any that have been heard elsewhere. Even in thought and feeling about the Eucharist the historian finds the same result. It is an Archbishop, enjoying continuity of order, who speaks of the sacrament in these pedestrian terms: 'Nor must I fail to remind you of that highly useful, and by no means terrible or difficult, duty of receiving the Lord's Supper.' It is Philip Doddridge, ordained without a bishop, who bids his flock to approach the sacred mysteries in language that shows more continuity with essential catholic devotion:

> *Hail, sacred feast that Jesus makes,*
> *Rich banquet of his flesh and blood.*

It is an echo (almost a translation) of St Thomas Aquinas in *Pange, lingua*:

> *Cibum turbae duodenae*
> *Se dat suis manibus.*

Doddridge continues:

> *Was not for you the Victim slain?*
>
> .   .   .   .   .
>
> *And may each soul salvation see*
> *That here its sacred pledges tastes.*

Victim and *pledges of salvation*: here is a continuity, than which none can be more important, in the most holy place with the most devout of all the centuries.

We have glanced at some results of an historical examination of one ecclesiastical problem; but what is true of the problem of continuity is true of many others. The approach through history, the study of men and women, what they were and what they did, can take away a hardness, a crudeness, an utterly unwarrantable confidence in the majesty of our own thought, which the historian seems to detect at times in the pronouncements of philosophers, scientists, mathematicians, and theologians. The main value of history is on the heart. It keeps the heart tender, as only a study of our poor humanity can.

This, which the historical approach can give, is never more needed than in the affairs of religion. Hardness of heart towards any man comes only from ignorance of him. There is no room for it among men who look together at a Divine Society which they believe to be the Body of Christ and pray in the same words: *Lord Jesus, King and Redeemer, save us by thy Blood.*

EPILOGUE

by Kenneth Slack

I<small>T</small> was appropriately at a shop on the steep slopes that lead up to Lincoln Cathedral that as a young R.A.F. chaplain I purchased *The Hymns of Wesley and Watts* by Bernard L. Manning, MA, Fellow of Jesus College, Cambridge. I had been using the *Methodist Hymnbook* and had begun to realize the greater treasures of the Wesleys' hymns than other collections reveal. Manning's short book performed the office of Philip to the Ethiopian eunuch. 'Understandest thou what thou readest?' Manning might have said to me. When I had read Manning on those hymns I realized their significance in making English religion what it was.

Then I suddenly recognized that this was the same man whose notices on the bursar's board at Jesus College had fascinated me in Cambridge days a little while before by their wit and pungency. Alas, I never met him. But since that discovery in 1942 I have searched for everything he ever wrote, and when I was called to rather unusual service of the Churches through the British Council of Churches I found myself reading and re-reading what he wrote. That itself may suggest a prophetic element in his writing.

What would Bernard Manning think of modern English religion almost four decades after he wrote this brilliant book? How would that mordant wit play upon the contemporary ecclesiastical scene, with its theological extemism and its widespread mood of frustration and defeatism? More important, how would he assess the vast changes coming over the religious aspect of our country, the increasing erosion at least of conventional religious activity and the apparent thrusting of the Churches more and more to the periphery of our society? How would he have reacted to the immense changes coming over church relations, most notably through the new openness of the Church of Rome towards 'the separated brethren,' but at many other points, too?

There was, of course, a strong element of conservatism in his nature, and therefore in his religion, the purest and fullest expression of his nature. It was tied up with a Roman sense of *pietas* towards the people and the institutions that had been a source of blessing to him. Caistor, Jesus College, Cambridge and his beloved Ravenstonedale high amidst the Westmorland moors—these evoked from him a loyalty as profound as his affection for them. For his father, George Manning, to whom he dedicated *Essays in Orthodox Dissent* and to whose memory he placed that lovely tablet in the High Chapel in Ravenstonedale where the elder Manning twice ministered, he had not only a filial love but a reverence towards a true minister of the Word.

This piety, derived from loyalty, reverence and affection, appears negatively in his damning reference to Mark Rutherford, as possessing 'such fame as moderate ability and immoderate disloyalty to domestic pieties will always command.'[1] To speak or write slightingly of our Holy Mother, the Church, was to Manning near to blasphemy.

David Edwards, in a recent address to the General Council of the Student Christian Movement, wisely reminds us that 'some highly educated people, including

1 *More Sermons of a Layman*, p. 139.

laymen such as T. S. Eliot or C. S. Lewis whom we have recently lost, have expressed their worship in conservative terms.' Bernard Manning was such a man, however far he was in other ways from the Tory, Royalist Anglo-Catholicism of a man like Eliot. Some part of this conservatism was due to the way in which he prized the upbringing he had had. Some part—and perhaps the more important from our point of view—came from his sense that a sentimental subjectivism in worship, churchmanship and theology was certain to prove desperately inadequate for the living of these days. Forty years on from this book who would fault him for that?

His love of the Scriptural, the objective and the restrained in hymnody has surely greatly influenced the two major hymn-books produced since the War, *Congregational Praise* and *The Baptist Hymn Book*, and may be expected to influence in similar degree the new Presbyterian hymnary which is in preparation. Possibly his influence has not been as wide upon new Anglican productions. This would not surprise Manning who remarked: 'The Anglican, because he has what Borrow justly called "England's sublime liturgy," has been careless of other liturgies, like the liturgy of hymns.'[1] Anyone who has striven to conduct worship with the aid of *Ancient and Modern Revised* will know what he means.

It is this element in Manning, the conviction that worship must express an objective faith rooted in the great saving acts of God recorded in Scripture, that would surely have made him rejoice at much of the effect of Biblical theology in the period that followed the publication of *The Making of Modern English*

1 *The Hymns of Wesley and Watts*, p. 134.

Religion. By the same token we cannot picture him as wholly happy about the 'new theology' commonly attributed to the South Bank and to that university which he graced and loved for so long. This is not to predicate to him a reactionary attitude. It is to suggest that he would have found some of the exaltation of the secular both unbalanced and humourless.

He had a strong sense of the need to enter into the actual situation in life of the people to whom the Gospel was being presented. Read his address on 'Effectual Preaching' given at the Yorkshire United Independent College, [1] and notably his description of the actual interests and emotions of those who are listening to a sermon and you will not doubt that. But this did not carry him to the absurd lengths to which some recent writers have gone in the attempt to identify themselves with secular man. His wit pricks the bubble of a good deal of intellectual pontificating on religion by the publicists of his day. 'Miss Rose Macaulay has now attained that age or that circulation at which popular novelists became omniscient; and like others of her class in that condition she has tried her prentice hand on religion.' [2] 'The enigmatical daughter of an old-fashioned rationalist recently wrote the biography of an ex-Quaker who had evaporated into a peculiarly precious highbrow .... What then does Virginia Woolf, in her life of Roger Fry, tell us about funerals?' [3] 'When you have allowed Dean Swift to delight you by the incomparable art of his richer wit, you find that, though Mr Sinclair Lewis and Mr Bertrand Russell are able to make it pretty clear that they, too, disapprove of most of us, their remarks

[1] *A Layman in the Ministry,* pp. 135–151.   [2] *The Hymns of Wesley and Watts,* p. 106.   [3] *More Sermons of a Layman,* p. 124.

can hardly be set beside his; theirs rank rather with the lucubrations of the Revd Mr Grundy in his parish magazine.'[1]

This is, of course, good clean fun, and designed to appeal to the undergraduate audiences to which many of his papers were read; but there is far more to it than that. He was reminding his first hearers, and can remind us, that the Church, while being humble, is not called upon to be a doormat for every man's trampling. He remarked somewhere that 'The situation is serious, but it does not call for the confession of sins that we have not committed.'

There is nothing of arrogance in Manning's writing on this kind of point. There is the scholar's love of accuracy and sense of proportion. There is also, more importantly, the sense of truth held in trust and experience that must not be denied. He was a Calvinist, but in no negative sense. It was not predestination that held him. It was the sovereignty of God. He referred in one of his finest addresses to the common conviction 'that evangelical religion is intellectually bankrupting, and that Calvinistic theology is morally revolting.'

'People still say that: Beachcomber in the *Daily Express* and more considerable theologians. When they find us unconvinced and, in our unregenerate moments, amused, they passionately assert that evangelical religion and Calvinistic theology are anyhow dead. We do not argue. We stand here with confidence, indeed with a certain consecrated truculence to speak that we know. The smoking flax is not quenched; the fire fallen from heaven is kindled afresh by the wind that bloweth where it listeth; the bush is not consumed.'[2]

1 *Essays in Orthodox Dissent*, p. 35.   2 *More Sermons of a Layman*, p. 141.

Manning would have sympathized with the missionary purpose of those theologians at present creating
what Canon Roger Lloyd has called 'The Ferment in
the Church'; [1] but he would probably have discerned
in their writings not a few of those perils of a liberalism
busy being emancipated from the supernatural and
identified with the world with which he broke a lance
in address after address given within the Congregational churches. It is true that his battle was against
an unscriptural and often sentimental modernism.
'The hymns are not paraphrases, nor are they charged
in every line with Scriptural content. They discuss
mountain scenery (with special attention to sunsets),
psychological disorders, priggish ambitions, and
political programmes. The preaching of the Word has
evaporated into flabby platitudes about the dangers of
the international situation or the benevolent common-
places of Ella Wheeler Wilcox expressed even more
prosaically than in her poetry.' [2] That is caricature,
maybe, but Manning felt it right to use every weapon
to fight what he regarded as a debilitating flabbiness in
the worship of his own tradition.

The danger today is different. The battle to recover
'orthodox dissent' in Congregationalism was won by
such men as Nathaniel Micklem at Mansfield College
and J. S. Whale at Cheshunt College. Manning was the
knight errant of the cause armed with a sharp lance
of wit, and with the strength of convictions founded
upon deep Puritan spirituality. Yet Manning would
certainly have challenged the emasculation of religion
by the removal of the supernatural, because he knew
the sources of a living and personal religion. What he

1 In a book of that title published in 1964.
2 *Essays in Orthodox Dissent*, p. 61.

writes in the closing chapter of this book about continuity in methods of devotion—'It exists not only in
liturgical forms of public worship, but even more in
the intimate contemplation of those things from which
passion and adoration spring'—gives us the clue.
Adoration was for him the heart of religion.

But it is perhaps in the field of unity that it is most
fascinating to speculate on Manning's possible judgement on the contemporary religious scene. His
'consecrated truculence' makes some of his writing
seem ambiguous on unity. The most obvious example
of this is in his attitude to the Church of England.

It would not be difficult to make an anthology of
anti-episcopal quotations from his writings. 'To accept
episcopacy at this stage of things, however "nice" a
reunion we may get at the price, means that we
unchurch the whole of the holy tradition which bred
us and that we throw on a new and more virile race of
Dissenters the onus of showing that in the dispensation
of grace in the Church there is no circumcision and no
uncircumcision whether it be called episcopacy or by
any other name.' On the same page he writes of the
South Indian scheme, which in 1947 was to lead to the
Church of South India, '*The disappearance of any churchmanship except episcopalian churchmanship:* that is the fact
of historic importance; and non-episcopalian churchmanship will have disappeared without English
episcopacy moving one inch from its legalistic position:
that is the tragic fact. A settlement in England on South
Indian lines would mean that the legalistic and
Judaic interpretation of churchmanship would be left
without a challenge here. Do we care about the liberty
of Christ's Church as little as that?'[1]

1 *Essays in Orthodox Dissent*, pp. 135–6.

This comes very near making non-episcopacy a mark of the Church; and it may be said today that the likelihood of the Church of England agreeing even to a 'South Indian' scheme within Britain is remote. Some of the vigour of Manning's dealing with Anglicanism may have sprung from his work on the history of *Protestant Dissenting Deputies*[1], recording as it does the well-nigh unbelievable treatment of Dissenters on questions such as burial rights well on into the nineteenth century. Some of the vigour may have come from the tug which the honest Dissenter often feels towards social and cultural assimilation with the Establishment in the older universities. But most of the vigour sprang from his sense of the liberty of Christ's Church and the necessity for the Church to avoid any legalistic bondage.

I described his attitude to unity as ambiguous. His biographer, Dr Frederick Brittain, quotes a letter which Manning wrote in answer to criticism of *Essays in Orthodox Dissent* on this point.

'I should be very sorry if I seemed to lack enthusiasm for reunion . . . . But I am afraid that some sorts of reunion will only mean a new schism and a harder task in future. I agree that some sort of episcopacy will probably be necessary for reunion; and it is precisely because, as a historian, I am tremendously impressed by the prestige of the institution that I am wary . . . . . Episcopacy has such prestige, such momentum, that I doubt my power or your power or our joint power to make it mean other than it means and has meant to all unreformed Christendom and to Anglo-Catholicism. Once we accept the fact of episcopacy, its momentum and prestige will let us in for that mechanical

1 Published posthumously in 1952.

Judaism which I can scarcely reconcile with Christianity. . . .

I agree that I am a traditionalist to the backbone, but of course tradition cuts both ways, and it is a great sacrifice of tradition for a Calvinist to go back on "parity of ministers".'[1]

Two comments may be made here. One is that Manning was deeply engaged in battling for the recovery of churchmanship within Dissent. *Essays in Orthodox Dissent* records many a foray in that battle. A slighter work, *Why not abandon the Church?*, being lectures given to Congregational young people, is a simpler statement of his basic conviction. 'Our Congregational churches are churches because they are part of the great Church, and only because of that. They are part of the one holy, catholic, apostolic, evangelical Church, that Church of which we say in the Creed: *I believe in the Holy Catholic Church*. They are not new, upstart, or poor relations of Anglicanism or Popery. Those are not older Churches than ours. They are not more authoritative than ours. There is only one Church. It was founded before the foundation of the world in God's eternal purpose.'[2]

The other comment is that the 'pipe-line' theory of apostolic succession which gave rise to Manning's strong fears that we should lose that 'grace which comes as God's free gift, not in legally restricted channels controlled by attorneys in episcopal robes'[3] is now abandoned by most serious Anglo-Catholic scholars. The emphasis on the episcopate as historic rather than apostolic, and the growing abandonment of any theology of grace which could be described as

[1] *Bernard Lord Manning: A Memoir*, p. 74.   [2] *op. cit.* p. 34.
[3] *Essays in Orthodox Dissent*, p. 142.

mechanical, would meet a great deal of Manning's concern. (I do not doubt that the correspondence columns of the *Church Times* would reveal tenacious holding to such positions; but if churches are to be judged by the letters to their journals who shall be saved?)

To present Manning as simply a harsh critic of Anglicanism would be lop-sided in the extreme. He had a deep love for the Church of England, and unbounded affection for its liturgy, *The Book of Common Prayer*. It is in one of his naughtier *jeux'd esprit*, a paper with the gloriously characteristic title and sub-title, 'Some Lapsed Dissenters: A Study in Ecclesiastical Pathology,' that he gives this moving and discerning description of the spirit of Anglicanism: 'Genuine Anglicanism is one of the finest things that this country has produced or can produce; I yield to no one in my affectionate appreciation of it; but it is like an English village or the Oxford manner or a sincere liking for roast beef and plum pudding. It is a growth of ages. More than one generation must contribute to it. Its essence is too strong and too delicate to be produced at will. The strong and beautiful and Christian part of Anglicanism is its unconscious part. As soon as it becomes self-conscious, it becomes strident and un-beautiful. The man who chooses to be an Anglican is by definition no Anglican. The Anglican does not choose: he occurs. Anglicanism is like many other good things: it is instinctive; you can lose it but you cannot concoct it.'[1]

We may judge therefore that he would consider a gap of thirty years between stage one and stage two of

1 Published posthumously in *The Congregational Quarterly* April, 1951, p. 159 *et seq.*

the Anglican-Methodist proposals as none too long for the conveying of a spirit at once so fine and so elusive! And we may equally judge—with some written evidence —that he would not be surprised that Methodism seems likely to accept a way of achieving inter-communion in stage one which would be unacceptable to the older Dissent. 'Because of their Anglican origin, they are peculiarly liable to be persuaded into accepting the yoke of legalistic episcopalianism . . . . without being quite aware of what is happening. We cannot doubt that the Anglicans will offer sooner or later very favourable terms to the Methodists. They would meet the Methodists everywhere, except on the fundamental issue. The Methodists would have to admit that full salvation comes by bishops alone—but anything else that they want they would get.'[1]

I do not myself see the present proposals in these terms—for what that is worth—but integrity in presenting Manning's likely judgement on the present religious scene demands that these words be quoted.

He would certainly feel far greater satisfaction in the much smaller act of union which seems now on the not too distant horizon between his own tradition and the Presbyterian Church of England. In 1933 he pleaded for it. An attempt was made to secure it after World War II. It failed. The reception being given to the document containing 'A statement of convictions on which a united Church, both catholic and reformed, might be built' prepared by the Joint Committee for Conversations between the Congregational Union of England and Wales and the Presbyterian Church of England is far more heartening. The Congregational reception of it, and the willingness of those churches

1 *Essays in Orthodox Dissent*, p. 145.

even now to give to the Union the character of a Congregational Church of England and Wales, are in some degree a monument to Manning's own tireless summoning of his fellow churchmen back to their classical reformed heritage.

'Personally,' wrote Manning in 1933, 'I have no doubt that union with Presbyterians is the next step. Having no sort of doubt whatever, I personally would pay almost any price to achieve that union. If I could work the oracle, I would bring it about tomorrow.'[1]

Manning was convinced that this was the next step for his own Church because 'Presbyterianism and Congregationalism are only two forms of the same thing; they are two forms of that great venture on a Church founded on grace, John Calvin's venture in Geneva. Presbyterianism is the centralized, Congregationalism is the decentralized, form of that venture. It was historical accident rather than principle which made us attempt the same task in different ways. You produce Presbyterianism or Congregationalism by using only a slightly different proportion of the same ingredients: we have to aim at securing the proportions fifty-fifty.'[2]

Manning would have rejoiced at the determination that such a union should be 'open-ended,' that is, a contribution towards a wider union; for his anxieties about union were based on a fear that a reformed churchmanship weakened by individualism and sentimentality would be unable to bring its true treasure to the coming great Church.

In regard to the new attitude of Rome towards other Churches it is not easy to speculate on Manning's judgement. Deeply devout as he was, we may be

1 *Essays in Orthodox Dissent,* p. 148. 2 ibid. p. 149.

certain that he would have responded to the spirit of
Pope John, and would have rejoiced in the signs of
renewal in worship and much else which are to be seen
in what he was wont naughtily to call Popery. After
a visit to the chapel where Hugh Benson, an Archbishop of Canterbury's son who became a Roman
priest, is buried he wrote to a friend: 'A most beautiful
chapel is built over the tomb—a chapel in which I
knew . . . . the power and reality of religion as I have
not known it for some years. There is in Roman
Catholicism at its best a simplicity of faith that makes
most of us seem very sophisticated men of good will.'[1]
A week later he wrote to the same friend: 'You need
not think that the scarlet woman has blandishments
to attract a simple Puritan like me. I only like the
fundamentally Christian parts of Rome, and those I
must be free to adore wherever I find them.'[2]

On the other side may be placed his deep fear that
the educational settlement of 1870 was a weapon
'presented to Roman Catholic clericalism.'[3] He
despised the cruder type of Protestant propaganda.
'But for all that the Roman danger is real. Democratic
institutions like ours give enormous power to a well-
organized block vote under effective control, as the
Roman vote is.'[4] Again he wrote, 'I have no fear of
Roman Catholics making the whole of our people
Roman Catholic. I should not object much if they
could make us all into good Roman Catholics. But they
can't do that. What they can do here in England is
what they have done everywhere else; they can make
half the people Roman Catholic and half anti-Christian.
By destroying evangelical religion here, they can give

---

1 and 2 *B. L. Manning: A Memoir*, p. 45.   3 *Protestant Dissenting
Deputies*, p. 353.   4 *Essays in Orthodox Dissent*, p. 129.

our people, as they give people on the Continent, no choice but a choice between clerical religion and anti-clerical materialism.'[1]

That the Roman Catholic proportion of the *worshipping* community (as opposed to statistics of nominal adherents) has grown since Manning wrote those words in 1931, there seems no room for doubt. Many would judge that that growth is so considerable as to begin to alter the religious balance of the country. Nor have the demands of the Roman Catholic Church for public funds for their own educational system abated. They may be expected to increase. What we may imagine Manning doing is rejoicing as the deeply religious man that he was in every release of new spiritual power in Rome, and yet watching with an historian's caution the actual implementing of, for example, the decree on religious liberty of the Vatican Council.

He would still have passionately asserted the truth and relevance of evangelical religion and reformed churchmanship. To read the opening chapters of the book to which this chapter is appended is to recognize how discerning a prophet Manning was about the continuing erosion and wasting of the medieval legacy. Earlier I have hazarded the guess that he would be far from happy with all the attempts of some theologians to accommodate the faith to the secular. But this is not to say that he would summon us to some retrogressive religion that behaved as though our world were other than it is. Rather we may say that just as he saw in the opening of the third chapter of this book that ... 'Creative forces have been at work. ... New springs of piety have been opened; or rather

1 *Essays in Orthodox Dissent*, p. 131.

the old springs have been approached by new direct ways that in a thousand years most men had forgotten,' . . . so he would expect renewal to come to the Church through the relevant recovery of evangelical religion in thought-forms and institutions meaningful for today.

Of one thing we may be sure. Manning would believe that whatever of renewal may come from our present ferment will depend upon the degree that God is seen as evoking adoration for what he has done in the Crucified.

INDEX